W9-BXL-621

YOU
NEED A
BUDGET

YOU NEED A BUDGET

The Proven System for Breaking the
Paycheck-to-Paycheck Cycle, Getting Out of
Debt, and Living the Life You Want

JESSE MECHAM

HARPER
BUSINESS

An Imprint of HarperCollins*Publishers*

YOU NEED A BUDGET. Copyright © 2017 by YNAB Licensing LLC. All rights reserved. Printed in the United States of America. No part of this book may be used or reproduced in any manner whatsoever without written permission except in the case of brief quotations embodied in critical articles and reviews. For information, address HarperCollins Publishers, 195 Broadway, New York, NY 10007.

HarperCollins books may be purchased for educational, business, or sales promotional use. For information, please email the Special Markets Department at SPsales@harpercollins.com.

FIRST EDITION

Library of Congress Cataloging-in-Publication Data has been applied for.

ISBN 978-0-06-256758-1

17 18 19 20 21   LSC   10 9 8 7 6 5 4 3 2 1

For Julie . . . and the six other small people
who live in our house.

Contents

YOU
NEED A
BUDGET

Introduction

If you're reading this book, money stresses you out in some way. For some of you it might be pull-your-hair-out stress. For others, maybe you just know your money situation isn't as good as it could be. Whether we're panicking or just feeling uneasy, money thoughts interrupt our peace of mind all the time, on so many levels. We usually don't even notice it happening.

You grab a $6 turkey sandwich at work, and while standing at the register you think of the stack of cold cuts in your fridge at home. "Should have gotten up earlier to pack lunch," you think. You read an article about how your generation isn't saving enough for retirement and wonder if you should up your 401(k) contribution. You save to remodel the bathroom and still worry it's the wrong move because your laptop is about to croak, the dog has a funny limp, and the growing rate of college tuition has us all thinking we should be eating beans between now and the time our kindergartners go to college. That tight feeling hits your chest, your breathing gets a little shallow, and you just chalk the stress up to your busy schedule.

Those little stress daggers are actually the same question on repeat: *Can I afford this?* And *this* can be as small as lunch out with friends, all the way up to retirement. The question haunts all of us, all the time—whether we're wealthy or broke, we're always wondering if we can afford something.

The only money question that rivals *Can I?* is its evil cousin: *Should I?* This one is partly fueled by our competitive nature, but mostly by not knowing what we really want. A colleague shares that he puts something away for his kids' college every month, and you wonder if you should do the same. Your cousin Instagrams her family's epic Disney trip (highlights reel only) and you think, "Should I go on vacation?"

Should I? always loops back to *Can I?*, keeping that anxiety bubbling so we know we need to do something—we're just not sure what, or when, or what we're even capable of.

Most of us feel paralyzed by this point and end up doing nothing, usually for one of three reasons:

We're not confident we know what is best. We're overwhelmed by options and have no idea whether to trust our gut, the guy yelling at us on TV, or something else entirely.

We don't have a system for making decisions. I'll talk a lot about this throughout the book, but the bottom line is that we need a system in place to drive our decisions. Without one, we're spending and saving on whims.

We're scared to learn the truth. Our finances are a black box. Money flies in and out of our accounts, and we guess we're doing fine because the balance never hits zero, but we have no idea what's truly going on. And we're afraid to find out.

What to do? How can you break the paralysis with so many factors keeping you in neutral? That's what this book will help you figure out. And my first, biggest piece of advice may jolt you out of any financial impasse:

Forget about the money.

Seriously. Because it's not about the money. Okay, it's about money a little bit. But money is not the point, not the end goal. In truth, when we're stressed about our finances, it's because we're not sure our money decisions are aligned with the life we want to be living.

The question we need to ask ourselves isn't *Can I?* or *Should I?* It's *What do I want my money to do for me?* Answering this question will help us cope with endless options, pressure to keep up with the Joneses, and the paralyzing fear that we're just not being smart with our money.

What do I want my money to do for me? works like a gut check that helps us see whether our priorities are driving our money decisions. When we know what we want our money to do for us, the options become a lot less daunting, and confidence quickly replaces the stress.

Gut Check: Go

What do I want my money to do for me?

In all the time you devote to working, spending, saving, and stressing, have you ever asked yourself this question?

Don't worry if you haven't. Most of us don't think about money in this way, and honestly, it's a hard question to answer. Not only that, but it's normal for your answer to change over time. That's why you need to keep doing the gut check with each money decision. It will either confirm your priorities or open your eyes to necessary changes.

Let me be clear: *What do I want?* and *What do I want my money to do for me?* are different questions. I'm not prompting you to write your holiday wish list. *What do I want my money to do for me?* is about nothing less than deciding what kind of life you want to live, and then making a plan so your money can help you get there.

If you're not already living the life you want, how would you like to live instead? Don't worry if your answer is radically different from your current reality. Just think about what's important to you. Maybe the life you want involves staying home with your kids, annual European vacations, going back to school, or just less stress around bills. It could be all of those things. It doesn't matter—the point is to decide what your priorities are, and then make a plan to meet them.

Without a plan, you're floating and stumbling, hoping life will someday click into place. It's a lot like going to college and never choosing a major (maybe you did that), or going grocery shopping and grabbing random things on the shelf hoping they'll add up to dinner (maybe you do that). This is actually how many of us treat our money. It just comes and goes without much thought until suddenly we are stressed, and we often don't even realize we're stressing about money. Everything just feels overwhelming.

The Antidote to Your Money Stress

That little life plan? It's actually a budget. Yes, a budget. You need one. I need one. We all need a budget—no matter how much money we have (or don't have). You picked up this book, so you probably already know that, but the idea of budgeting may still scare you. If you're worried it will be too rigid, restricting, and unforgiving, it's time to look at budgeting from a different angle. Forget about the things you *can't* do with your money (*I can't afford that trip*), or the things you *have* to do with your money (*I have to pay off my student loans*). Instead, think of what you *want*, and go from there. *I want to take my family to Italy. I want to live debt-free. I want to hire a personal tutor to learn Italian.* A budget lets you plan for all of these things.

I mentioned earlier that many of us struggle with money choices because we don't have a system for making decisions. Your budget is that system. It's a tool for designing your life around *what you want*. Without a budget you have no way to prioritize your spending. You often don't even know where your money is truly going. You may stress about not being able to afford what's important to you while you simultaneously spend on things you'd willingly nix if you could see the trade-offs. That's the beauty of a (good) budget: it lets you see *exactly* how your spending affects the rest of your life.

Perhaps that trip to Italy seems beyond your reality. Meanwhile, the takeout habit you barely enjoy costs you hundreds a month. You might fill your closet with eBay impulse buys you rarely wear while you cringe at your student loan balance.

If you've been wondering how you'll ever afford to (fill in the blank), you may not have to look as far as you think. This is what makes budgeting actually fun and liberating. There's nothing like the joy of zapping meaningless expenses and putting those dollars toward something that once seemed like a pipe dream. Imagine seeing your vacation fund grow while your waistline shrinks (double whammy!), or seeing your student debt disappear as your clutter subsides.

When the dollars stop leaving on a whim, you can make sure they fuel the things you *do* care about before they walk away. Your budget lets you spend and save guilt-free because you've already decided where you want those dollars to go. It helps you look at your money through a whole new lens, so that you always feel good about your decisions—whether you're spending or not spending.

This will play out differently for everyone. After taking a close look at your spending, you may decide takeout and eBay purchases *are* important to you—just maybe not as important as saving for Italy or paying off your loans. Whatever you decide, you can find a way to fund anything that, to you, makes for a good life. You just need a plan.

Meet YNAB's Four Rules

This book will arm you with two very powerful—and personal—tools by the time you're done reading:

A **concrete system** for making financial decisions tailored to the life you want. That system is your budget.

A **new mindset** for looking at your money in ways you never have before. That mindset is YNAB's Four Rules.

I'll spend the rest of this book unpacking the Four Rules and showing you how YNABers (that is, people who use YNAB) have used those rules to transform their lives. Here's the aerial view to start:

Rule One: Give Every Dollar a Job, is all about being *proactive*, so life doesn't simply claim your money. Instead, you'll decide on priorities first, then assign dollars (only the ones you have right now—we'll talk a lot about this!) to those priorities before they walk off. Because your money is going toward your highest priorities, your spending has to clear a higher bar.

Rule Two: Embrace Your True Expenses, combines the power of thinking ahead with taking action here and now. Whether expenses happen like clockwork (rent), feel impossible to predict (car repairs), or are just far-off dreams (cash for a wedding), they are all part of your true expenses. The key is to prepare a bit at a time by treating them all like monthly expenses.

Rule Three: Roll with the Punches, helps you adapt so you can handle whatever comes your way. Your budget is a plan—but plans change, and your budget should, too. Spend more than you expected on dinner out with friends? Life throw you a curveball? No need for stress. Just pull some money from lower-priority categories and carry on. You haven't failed at budgeting, you've adapted with the best of them. This flexibility isn't how most people imagine a budget, but it may be the key to making it work.

Rule Four: Age Your Money, gets you working toward spending money you earned at least thirty days ago. When you increase the time that passes between receiving your money and spending it, you're more secure, more flexible. You're breathing easier. If you're implementing the first three rules, you'll be aging your money before you know it, and you can officially say good riddance to the paycheck-to-paycheck cycle. (Don't let the door hit you on the way out!)

These Four Rules work for anyone, no matter what your income level or goals might be. It doesn't matter if you're a recent grad navigating your first year of adulting or a retiree just starting to make withdrawals from your 401(k). Rich or poor, frugal or a spendthrift, the Four Rules will help you proactively engage with your money every day so you're in control of your finances.

Before There Were Four Rules, There Were Two Newlyweds

I started You Need a Budget (YNAB) in 2004 because my wife, Julie, and I were desperate. We were twenty-two-year-old newlyweds living in the 300-square-foot basement of a sixty-year-old house. We were both students "living on love." But love doesn't pay for your college tuition, books, or bus pass. (Did I mention we didn't own a car?) I was three years away from finishing my master's degree in accounting, so earning an actual salary was not in my near future. Julie was wrapping up her bachelor's degree in social work, and began working for—wait for it—$10.50 an hour.

On top of that, we were planning for our first child and there was no way we could afford to live our dream of having Julie become a stay-at-home mom. I was feeling desperate, but as a numbers nerd, I knew I'd find the answer in an Excel spreadsheet (where all of life's magic happens). So I began developing a system to help us track our expenses.

My idea was simple. I planned to record everything we spent. Each of the spreadsheet's rows represented a day of the year. All of our spending and saving categories were lined up across the top. I had included the usual: groceries, textbooks, eating out, phone, gasoline, etc. The budget was beautiful to me in the way that any ordinary thing is always beautiful in the eyes of its creator.

Julie and I stuck to using the budget daily, and after a couple of months, something surprising happened. Despite our meager financial circumstances, we realized we were doing pretty well. We could pay our bills and even put a little money aside. We still did all of the things that, to us, made for a good life. We budgeted for a few date nights each month, going out with friends, and a little spending money for each of us. We weren't living paycheck to paycheck and we were hitting our goals. The budget had been working.

So I did some thinking. If my budgeting strategies had worked for me, maybe they could work for other people, too.

At this point we were eager to bring in more money so we could achieve our goal of having Julie be a stay-at-home mom. I started thinking that I could bring in extra income beyond my hourly intern work to give us even more breathing room as we transitioned Julie out of the workforce. My idea was to convince people that a budget would also work for them. YNAB was born.

As I began teaching people the principles that had helped Julie and me, I saw that what we had was pretty special. We were following four basic but powerful rules and they had changed our finances forever. We didn't fight about money. We felt content (even with our extremely small income).

Fast-forward a decade and these same rules have helped hundreds of thousands of individuals and families all over the world. I did end up with a master's in accountancy and became a licensed CPA, but I shunned the spotlight of CPA stardom and decided to launch You Need a Budget into a full-fledged business. My full-time work—and this entire book—is focused on helping you realize that financial freedom can be yours as well. But to get it, you need a budget.

Hang with me. You've never budgeted like this.

Let's Get a Couple of Things Straight

I want to be clear about a few things before we go any further:

I won't ever tell you what to do with your money. Yes, this is a personal finance book, but it doesn't matter. It's not my place to tell you whether your money should be in the stock market, in your savings account, or on your feet in the form of a new pair of Air Jordans (which color did you go with?). You're the only person who can know what your money needs to do for you, because your priorities are *yours*. But figuring out what you want your money to do can be the hardest part, and that's what I'm here to help you accomplish. Your goals and priorities will also probably change over time. That's normal. It all depends on what you want your life to look like.

You don't need to subscribe to YNAB's online budgeting software. If you can't already tell, YNAB is more about your money mindset than it is about how you choose to track your dollars. Whether you've been using YNAB's software for years or you prefer to track your progress with paper and pencil, YNAB's Four Rules will still apply. Give some thought to how you'll be most comfortable tracking your budget. Excel brings me a certain joy I can't fully explain, so Julie and I happily rocked our YNAB spreadsheet for years. If you prefer paper, you may thrive by budgeting with a simple notebook. You'll be engaging with your budget often, so make sure the tracking method you choose gels with your personality. On that note . . .

This is not a set-it-and-forget-it approach. Some money management guides (books, software, psychics, whatever!) make it so you can allegedly put everything on autopilot. That's great when it comes to paying bills, but YNAB is about so much more than that. If you're ready to design the life you want, you'll need to engage with your money *consistently*. Every time money hits your bank account you'll set a plan for those dollars. Every purchase you make will be backed by the decision that this is actually how you want to spend those dollars.

Anytime you go rogue with your spending you'll adjust your plan to stay on track with your goals.

I did say earlier that it's not about the money, and it's not. It's about your priorities. But you *do* need to pay close attention to what you're doing with your money so it supports your priorities. YNAB gets you to be very intentional with your money—the complete opposite of autopilot—but I think you'll find you won't mind putting in the extra time and energy once you start seeing everything you can accomplish.

Before you crack open your bank account, let's draw the curtain on the new mindset that's about to upend the way you view your money.

A CHEAT SHEET TO RELIEVING
YOUR MONEY STRESS

Most of our money stress swirls around two debilitating questions: *Can I?* and *Should I?* Forget both questions, because they'll never help you make good money decisions. Instead, ask yourself: *What do I want my money to do for me?* Once you do this, you're letting your priorities drive your choices.

The real secret sauce to making sure your money is moving you toward the life you want is YNAB's Four Rules. If you embrace budgeting they'll be emblazoned on your brain in short order:

- Rule One: Give Every Dollar a Job
- Rule Two: Embrace Your True Expenses
- Rule Three: Roll with the Punches
- Rule Four: Age Your Money

Now get ready—you'll never see your money the same way again.

CHAPTER 1:

A New Way to Look at Your Money

If you care enough about money to be reading this book, there's a chance you've tried to budget before. For most of us, that exercise has gone something like this:

We open an Excel spreadsheet and create rows for our spending categories—I mean, that's what I did. We start listing things we spend money on, but there isn't a lot of order to it. We get the nonnegotiables like rent, loans, car, utilities. We mix in other expenses, small and large alike, and because someone told us this is what it means to be responsible adults, we add something about savings and even a vacation fund.

Once we have our beautiful list of expenses, we fill every line item with dollar amounts based on *what we think we will—or should—spend* in any given month. Many nonnegotiables are easy since they're the same recurring amount, and we can ballpark a pretty accurate number for things like utilities. For the rest, we plug in what we feel are generous but not-too-crazy numbers because this is a budget, not a free-for-all.

When we're done, we admire our handiwork. Even though it has holes in it, it's more than we've done before, and so we lay out a plan to follow it every month. It feels so good to know exactly where our future paychecks need to go.

But what happened after you made that gorgeous spreadsheet? My guess is that you abandoned it pretty quickly. My friends Nikki and Aaron were excited about theirs, but they gave up within a month when they discovered their actual spending looked nothing like the numbers in those Excel boxes. They were overwhelmed by the disparity and decided to revisit budgeting when life got a little calmer (spoiler alert: that never happens). My neighbor Summer told me she ditched her budget because she never had enough cash to fund every line item she'd so optimistically planned. That reality made her want to avoid her spreadsheet like it was her ex-mother-in-law (both uncannily made her feel like she was never "enough"). She gave up, figuring that either budgeting didn't work or she just wasn't good with money.

If this scenario sounds painfully familiar, don't worry. It's not you. It's a flawed system.

That kind of budgeting doesn't work for a few reasons. First, there is no room for prioritizing. Every line item competes for your dollars and there's no structure to decide what should get funded first. There's also no structure to make sure important things aren't *left out*. You probably (hopefully) give bills and life essentials top priority. But how will you decide what gets cash next, especially if you don't have enough for everything? Put more toward your student loan balance, or save for vacation? Dump money into your daughter's 529 or save up for her summer camp? Cue the running and screaming.

It also offers zero flexibility. You automatically fail the moment real life doesn't align with your predictions. Who wants that kind of stress?

Another big problem is that this is not actually budgeting, it's **forecasting**. Forecasting is when you look into the future and guess at your upcoming income and spending. This can be fun because we're painting a picture of the life we want to live, or the person we want to be, without having to worry just yet about making those numbers work. It's easy to throw $300 into your vacation fund and $500 into your grocery allowance when you're talking about future money. The reverse approach is also a problem: You can swear you'll only spend $50 a month on groceries, but that never happens in real life and you end up feeling bad just for buying your family's essentials.

The difference between forecasting and budgeting is a lot like the difference between dreaming and doing. It's fun to forecast and *dream* of the life you want if you can someday get those numbers to work. But how about looking at the money you have right now and creating a spending plan based on what's most important to you? That's what YNAB is all about.

When you view your money through this lens—prioritizing the money you *have right now*—the whole picture changes. Now you're not just guessing and hoping—you're being intentional with your dollars. You're letting your priorities drive how you spend the money you have on hand. And you're forgetting about any promise of future money.

Hear me out: I'm not saying you shouldn't think about the future. Your budget is all about thinking ahead. Just make sure you don't forecast *future money*. That cash will be great when it hits your account, but you're only concerned with making sure the money you have *today* gets you closer to your goals.

This shift is a big deal. It's the difference between dreaming about a better life and actually creating one. The moment you let your priorities lead, you'll find that many of your anxieties around money—and the jitters you thought weren't about money at all—quickly disappear. The fog clears and you can see exactly where you're going.

This is precisely what happened to Julie and me when we started budgeting. We went from wondering how we'd ever afford to become a single-income household with kids to seeing *exactly* how it was going to happen. In our case it involved extreme feats in nonspending, but that's only because we were trying to accomplish so much on a tiny income. Our budget was so simple that I still remember it exactly. At the time we were bringing in just under $1,900 a month between the two of us, which we put toward the following priorities:

$350 rent (which included utilities—even a landline!)
$120 groceries
$15 annual car registration
$75 gas

$10 fun money ($5 for each of us)

$25 eating out

$125 school textbooks

$130 health insurance

$25 hair care/toiletries

$120 saving for new car

$45 Christmas

$550 savings (so Julie could be a SAHM once our first baby came, and I could finish school)

Your budgeting reality may look very different from what ours was, but the same principles apply. Just look at the money you have on hand today and decide what you want those dollars to do for you. This is YNAB's first rule—Give Every Dollar a Job.

(If you're already starting to think about money you don't have yet, remember, the big shift is to focus *only* on what you have today. Let go. Try it.)

Let's say you have $400 in your checking account today. You know your $50 cell phone bill and $100 cable bill are due before you get paid again, so you earmark those funds. You also have plans to cook dinner for Evelyn, the girl you just started dating, but your fridge contains exactly six eggs, a carton of half-and-half, and a coconut. You assign $100 for dinner ingredients and a bouquet of flowers. You still have $150 left, which is great because you're going out for your brother's birthday tomorrow night. You think it will be fine because your account balance looks decent. Except, you seriously have six eggs, a carton of half-and-half, and a coconut in your fridge. You need to buy yourself some food. Just as you split your remaining dollars between groceries ($100) and going out ($50), you realize you haven't allocated anything toward your goal of paying down your credit card debt. The bill is due next week so you have to pull from that $400 if you want to keep up with your debt goal this month.

Yikes, money suddenly feels kind of scarce. Don't worry, and don't quit budgeting—this feeling of scarcity is a good thing. It means you're seeing your money for what it truly is: a finite resource—and this is a huge part of that mindset shift I talked about. It doesn't actually matter how much money we have or don't have. Scarcity is simply that feeling of *wishing there were more*. This is an important moment. The feeling of scarcity might tempt us to quit, but when we step back and embrace scarcity, we make good decisions. When we recognize our dollars are finite, we're more intentional about how we spend them. Scarcity pushes us to be very concrete about our priorities, and those that matter to us the most make themselves known in these moments. And that will help make significant changes for the better with your finances. But I'm getting ahead.

Here's the challenge: It feels like everything vying for that $400 is a priority to you. You've wanted to show Evelyn your cooking skills since you first connected over your love of *Top Chef*. There's simply no way you're canceling dinner. Spending time with family is a top priority and you'd never miss your brother's birthday. You can't skip eating for the rest of the

month (really, don't try it). And you decided last year that you
really want to dig yourself out of debt before you get married.
(You didn't even have a girlfriend back then—a girl like Evelyn
was just a dream. Don't mess it up!) What to do?

Money is scarce but you know that if you're hyperinten-
tional about your spending you can stretch that $400 over each
of those top priorities. So you revise the dinner menu with Evelyn from surf-and-turf to roast chicken and hit the sale circu-
lar for your own groceries. You also decide what you'll spend
for your brother's birthday before leaving the house. You happily stick to the birthday budget because you know that spending more would make you miss the credit card goals that are so
important to you. These changes free up the $150 you need for
your debt payment goal. Success! Here's the aerial view:

$400, take one:	$400, take two:
$50 cell phone	$50 cell phone
$100 cable	$100 cable
$100 dinner date	$35 dinner date
$100 groceries	$35 groceries
$50 going out	$30 going out
	$150 debt payment

Had you not budgeted, that $400 checking account balance
would have seemed like more than enough to carry you to the
next paycheck. You would have spent it blindly, not realizing
that the money you burned on a cab to your brother's party
really needed to fund your lunch for the next two weeks. You
also wouldn't have known—until it was too late—that the

aged steaks you bought to impress Evelyn ultimately kept you from your debt-paydown goal. By being intentional with your spending, you managed to fuel all of your priorities with no financial fallout.

Now you're making real decisions with your money, and your priorities are shining through.

IS IT BUDGETING, OR IS IT FORECASTING?

The difference between budgeting and forecasting can seem murky if you're just starting out. If rent isn't due for two weeks, but your next paycheck will land before then, are you forecasting by relying on that future check? Not at all—as long as you don't budget for rent until you have the money.

If you don't have enough to budget out the rest of the month, then budget for things based on 1) their importance and 2) their sequence. So if you have $200 and you need to buy food, budget for that before budgeting for the rent that is due in two weeks. As soon as the next paycheck arrives, cover rent and any other essentials that are immediately due. If this leaves you really short and worried, you get creative. You need more money, so you cut, you sell, you earn. That's when you're really taking control.

That said, the goal of the Four Rules is to get you to the point where you are never timing bills to paychecks. That may feel impossible, but you *can* get there. Just keep your eyes on your priorities—and keep reading.

Use Your Budget to Write Your Future

As I said earlier, there's nothing wrong with looking to the future. YNAB's Rule Two: Embrace Your True Expenses, is all about anticipating future expenses, and this is especially important for people with a fluctuating income. Just don't confuse budgeting with forecasting—one is a real-life plan, the other is a series of guesses built on what-ifs and maybes. Forecasting has you "budgeting" money you don't have and pretending you know exactly what your expenses will be three months from now. You know it probably won't work out that way, and you don't feel much better after you've run the imaginary numbers. Budgeting has you prioritizing the money you have—and leaves you feeling confident because you know it's one hundred percent based in reality.

Don't worry; "based in reality" isn't code for painfully modest or restricting. The opposite is actually true. Budgeting helps you see where your money is truly going so you can reroute it if it's not going in the places you want. So if you want to go to Paris, go to Paris! If you decide you really need to buy a beach house, buy one! But actually budget for these things so you can fund your dream soon—don't just hope that you can someday afford it while the years, and dollars, slip away.

Phil and Alexis converted their "someday dream" into reality when they started budgeting in January 2015. Alexis was planning to quit her job that spring to become a freelance Web designer and spend more time with their three-year-old son,

Jack. I love their story because it shows exactly how budgeting helped them in the moment *and* helped them look down the road with confidence. Before Alexis could find the nerve to quit her nine-to-five job, she wanted to figure out how long the $20,000 "freelance fund"—which they'd taken two years to save—would cover their lifestyle in the Boston suburbs. The goal was for their savings to cover all expenses because they didn't want to assume Phil's salaried paycheck (he's a designer at an ad agency) would always be there. With Alexis quitting, they'd be financially devastated if Phil's income suddenly vanished in a wave of layoffs.

They hadn't budgeted until now, but they had a good sense of their spending patterns after the two-year quest to save up that freelance fund. So they budgeted for fixed expenses and essentials, plus the few remaining add-ons that were important to them: a weekly date night, vacation fund, toddler music classes, and a little miscellaneous spending for breathing room. Other new expenses were also on the horizon: Jack's preschool tuition and the monthly payment on their new furnace since the heater that came with their house died last month.

When Phil and Alexis saw that their $20,000 freelance fund would only cover three months of expenses, their blood went cold. They really wanted the peace of mind in knowing that they had enough for the next six months, no matter what happened. That would give Alexis enough time to build a client base, and it would let them put Phil's paychecks in savings to help fund future months.

They knew something had to change and they were willing

to adjust their lifestyle so they could afford to have Alexis go freelance. It was a priority for them to have a parent in the family who wasn't tied to an office. They needed the flexibility so Alexis could take Jack to and from preschool when he started in the fall. She was also looking forward to spending more time with Jack rather than being stuck at the office. Until this point, they were blessed to have Alexis's parents watch Jack full-time for free. Preschool tuition was a significant bill, and it was hitting their budget just when Alexis's predictable income was about to vanish. But they were determined to make Operation Alexis Goes Freelance a reality.

So they revisited the budget, got real about their priorities, and shaved $870 from their monthly expenses within a few minutes: eating out went down by $250 and babysitters by $150. They would still have their date nights, but they decided to cook a special meal at home two Fridays a month after Jack went to bed. They didn't mind downgrading their $150 cable plan to an $80 plan since they rarely watched most of those extra channels ($70 savings). And while they were proud to be putting $400 a month into Jack's college fund, they agreed it was worth freezing those payments temporarily until their family was on firmer financial ground.

After nixing those expenses, they also *added* $150 a month to start saving for basement repairs. They'd noticed water leaking through a crack in their foundation during the last big rainstorm and were told they'd need to patch it up within the next year. They dreaded the idea of having to rush the repairs if another big storm hit. They didn't love adding an expense to their budget, especially now, but it would be way worse to have to find the full amount unexpectedly. Saving in installments was a big stress reliever.

They still had work to do if they wanted to stretch that $20,000 for a full six months, but things were starting to look brighter. They could see a way to their goals.

This looks a lot like forecasting, but there's a key difference: Alexis and Phil made their plans based only on the $20,000 they already had. They didn't play with nebulous numbers— they set a concrete plan for the real cash sitting in their bank account, based on their priorities. Once they were aware of what their money needed to do so they could live the life they wanted, the changes weren't as difficult as they'd thought. Knowing they had enough for groceries over the next six months trumped frequent dinners out. Padding their mortgage fund felt so much better than paying for six different MTV channels. Budgeting helped them get crystal-clear focus on their priorities, and those priorities now drive every one of their spending decisions.

KNOW WHEN TO LISTEN TO GUILT

The idea of doing *whatever you want* with your money can make some people uncomfortable. Guilt quickly creeps in if we worry that the priorities we've chosen may not be the best use of our money. How can you justify saving (and then spending) thousands on the fireplace of your dreams, or a week at Disney, when you imagine that a "smarter" person might use that money to, say, invest in the stock market? Smaller choices aren't spared, either. Should you really be spending on monthly pedicures or lunch with friends? It depends.

If guilt haunts you it's usually because:

1. You know in your gut that a bigger priority needs more of your attention; or

2. You're letting other people's expectations of how you should live your life color your choices.

This is where budgeting and soul-searching quickly intersect. Budgeting eventually even *becomes* soul-searching. It's why I dedicate the entire next chapter to helping you uncover your priorities. You won't feel confident about your money decisions unless you dig deep to figure out what really matters to *you*. It takes work to silence your inner critic and do what makes you happy. But once you find the courage to do it, you'll never want to go back.

This Is What Happens When You're Living the Life You Want

A funny thing happens when you start to follow YNAB's Four Rules. Every dollar you possess is accompanied by a little power jolt. You feel totally in control of your money, and your life.

A latte is no longer just a latte. It's financial freedom (stay with me here—it really is).

When you spend on a budget, that latte is a purchase you've

decided to make because you want to, and because you can, guilt-free. If you're saving (or, rather, refraining from buying), you're doing it with conviction, not just because "lattes are so expensive." Guilt-free there, too.

When you ask, *What do I want my money to do for me?* you're deciding how you'll use your money to get closer to the life you want. If going out for coffee brings a certain joy to your day that you don't want to lose, build a coffee category into your budget and don't feel bad when you buy one! Just make sure the coffee is actually helping to bring you closer to your goals. Maybe it is if you've decided that the few minutes of social time with your coworkers is important to you. Or if it means a lot for you to take fifteen minutes out of a hectic day to enjoy something you love.

Once your goals are in place, they back up every one of your spending moves. If you've decided it would bring you peace of mind to have a $20,000 emergency fund and you want to save $1,000 a month until you hit your goal, you'll happily adjust your spending behavior to make it happen. Maybe part of your saving strategy will be no more lattes, but it doesn't have to be *if you love lattes.*

Of course, making a plan for your money goes well beyond funding your caffeine fix. It puts you in control of your money before it—or the lack of it—has a chance to control you. This is the driving force behind Rule Two: Embrace Your True Expenses. By breaking large, infrequent expenses into smaller, frequent milestones, you're getting rid of "surprise" bills that tend to blindside us. Suddenly, they aren't surprises.

Budgeting is what allowed Phil and Alexis to launch Alexis's office-free life. By being more intentional with every dollar that left their account—or didn't—they were able to stretch their freelance fund for months longer than their prior spending habits would have allowed. And because Alexis was no longer sweating over how they'd get by, she had the mental clarity to put more energy into building her client base. This meant she wouldn't even need to rely on their freelance fund for very long.

If you're not planning, you're tossing money at things as they land in front of you—whether those things are bills or desires—and just hoping you'll have some left when the dust settles. With budgeting, on the other hand, you're mapping out your spending decisions before they happen. You can plan for the unplanned, even if the "unplanned" is just for fun. For example, impulse purchases typically get a bad rap, but why do they have to? Maybe the occasional clearance rack purchase brings you a thrill and you're worried that budgeting means you can no longer troll the Anthropologie sale during your lunch break. Well, if you've met all your essentials and there's money left over, why not actually budget for a few impulse buys every month? As a bonus, you won't feel guilty about spending the money, because its actual purpose is to fund your shopping trip. *That's why it's there!* And if you don't have anything in your "impulse buy" category this month, you'll know it's because you intentionally put your dollars toward something else—a different priority that's more important to you. You're in control.

When you decide what you want your money to do for you, you're no longer wondering, "Can I afford this?" That's a good question—you do need to make sure you have the cash before you use it—but the bigger question is, *Does this move me closer to my goal?* When *that's* the filter guiding your money decisions, each dollar becomes a lot more powerful.

Get Ready for Financial Freedom

Your new YNAB money mindset has a lot of perks. The buzz that comes with budgeting and hitting your goals rarely subsides. Each time we set a plan for our money and stick with it, or we pivot with the unexpected, we feel amazing. That's because most of us don't realize how much we were stressing about money until the stress goes away.

As the anxiety dwindles, something much better takes its place: peace. Imagine paying your bills the moment they land because the money is just there, actually waiting for the bill. (Personally, I get a little thrill when I come home to a pile of bills I can pay on the spot.) Imagine shopping without guilt, saving without drudgery, and feeling that you can literally plan to live in whatever way makes you happy. Your crazy dreams suddenly don't seem so crazy when you have a way to make them real.

This, to me, is financial freedom. It's a way of never having to worry about money even if you don't have endless piles of it. You don't have to be Scrooge McDuck, swimming through a pool of gold coins, to experience financial freedom. (But if that's your goal, hey, go for it.) You just need to make a plan for your money so it's doing exactly what you want it to do.

YOUR NEW MONEY MINDSET IN ONE SENTENCE:

Forget future money; use today's money to write your future.

CHAPTER 2:

Rule One—Give Every Dollar a Job

Rule One: Give Every Dollar a Job sounds simple enough, and it is. Just check your bank account balance and assign a job to every dollar you own. You're officially budgeting the moment you start doing this, and with every "job" you assign you're answering the question: *What do I want my money to do for me?*

Before you can start bossing your dollars around, though, you have to decide what needs to get done. You're literally writing a to-do list for your money. If you've never done something so (pro)active with your money, you'll quickly see how it changes your perspective on each dollar you hold.

Start with your survival. I know I said I wouldn't tell you what to do with your money, but I'm going to break my own rule here and say that if your basic well-being isn't your top priority, you should change your plan. That cruise is a pipe dream if you don't know where you stand with the basics that make you a functioning member of society.

Write down all of the places your money *needs* to go. Focus on payments you're obligated to make to keep your life running. Think food and shelter, loans, school payments, and any necessary work expenses (for example, an Internet connection if you work from home, commuting costs, etc.). YNABers Lia and Adam set these categories as their core obligations:

Rent	Car payment
Natural gas	Fuel
Electricity	Car repairs
Internet	Car insurance
Phones	Life insurance
Groceries/toiletries	Student loans
	Wedding debt

Rule One gets personal, fast. We all need to start with our obligations, but even those vary drastically from person to person. Maybe your mortgage is paid off and you walk to work. Your obligations will already look way different from Lia and Adam's.

Once you have your priority list, start doling out jobs. Start today, with whatever you have in your bank account. Ask yourself: *What do I need this money to do before I get paid again?* Is your rent or mortgage due this week? A credit card bill? School tuition?

Again, fund your obligations before you do anything else. If you're setting up your first budget, don't even think about funding other spending areas—not yet. Just make sure you've set aside enough to keep food in your fridge, a roof over your head, and the collection agencies off your porch. Planning for anything else will be a lot more fun when you know the essentials are covered (unless you get a thrill out of wondering whether your lights will get turned off—I knew a guy like that in college).

The rest of your priorities take over after your obligations are funded. This is where budgeting gets exciting. You'll quickly jump from paying your bills to mapping out a plan for the life you want to live. You'll no longer just spend or save on a whim. You'll be doing it with intention, and you'll make sure the things that are most important to you get priority over your dollars.

Challenge Every Assumption

As you consider your obligations, keep in mind that you have more control over these expenses than you may realize. Some things, such as debt payments, are not very flexible, but you have a lot of creative freedom to design your expenses around the kind of life you want to live.

To start, make sure you're separating honest-to-goodness *obligations* from habits disguised as necessities. It can be hard to distinguish between the two at times. Just remember that your habits are ultimately negotiable in a pinch—your obligations are not. You could come up with an alternate plan for buying lunch if you really needed to. Paying your rent or mortgage? Not as easy to get around unless moving in with your parents is on the table. No shame.

We can fall into the trap of thinking certain expenses just are what they are—but that's rarely the case. You can almost always do something to shrink your spending. This is where challenging every assumption can make a big impact on your budget. It's also a great time to consider how certain changes may improve your quality of life—after all, your budget is about making change for the better.

Is your car an obligation? Maybe it is right now because you need it to drive to work and public transportation isn't an option. But can you move closer to work and bike or walk? While you're at it, can you move to a smaller, cheaper house that also costs less to heat and cool? If you have two cars, can you get by with one? It may sound crazy to consider such big-picture changes, but maybe not. It depends on what a good life looks like to you.

Julie and I moved our family to a smaller house just after our sixth child, Faye, was born. When shopping for our first home, we were convinced we needed a big dining room because we love to entertain. Turns out, at least in Utah, you can't get a big dining room without the extra bedrooms and huge living room to complete the package. There was a lot to love about our home—fun neighbors, close to everything—but we realized we didn't need so much house. Everyone piled into the kitchen during parties and our kids like keeping each other company by sharing bedrooms (ask them again when they're teenagers, but they'll just have to work it out). We "traded down" in terms of house size but the new place came with other intangibles that were important to us: less traffic, more privacy, and epic views of Utah Valley. Getting costs down and quality of life up felt like a big win for us.

Challenging your assumptions doesn't have to mean huge life changes. Even minimal effort can save you money without disrupting your day-to-day. Look at your bills. Perhaps your cell phone is an obligation because you need it for work. But can you switch to a cheaper data plan? Maybe you could if you made sure to connect to Wi-Fi whenever you're home. Also be careful about grouping certain bills with other top priorities. Do you need Netflix *and* Hulu *and* cable? Maybe not, but if you lump them all into TV it's easy to overlook the potential excess.

This isn't about depriving yourself. The point is to question your habitual reactions to what you assume are obligations. Take a step back so you can see them with total clarity. You may find you absolutely need to pay as much as you're paying. But you'll often be surprised to discover how much is truly flexible.

Try letting stress be your barometer here. If you're stressing over high bills, find ways to scale back until you have (what you feel is) a comfortable margin between what you earn and what you spend. But keep watching—it's possible to go too far. If you *never* spend to the point of feeling deprived, that's also stressful. It will take time to find your sweet spot, and even that may shift. Just try to stay aware of your stress levels, of how much your money is really doing what you want it to, and adjust accordingly.

Spoiler Alert: Embrace Your True Expenses

We can't talk about obligations without jumping ahead to Rule Two: Embrace Your True Expenses. Chapter 3 offers a deep dive into Rule Two. For now it's enough to say that your obligations go beyond your monthly bills and essentials—recognizing this was key for Julie and me, and will be for you, too. Before you can set aside money for other priorities, it's important to freeze some funds for longer-term obligations. Think of the car insurance bill that has a way of showing up every six months, or the water bill that slithers into your mailbox every three months—always out of the blue, *always* when you just thought you were getting ahead.

Rule Two prompts you to break those bigger expenses into monthly installments so you're prepared to pay them when they hit. When you do this, big expenses don't feel so big, and you're never blindsided. Because let's face it: you know when your car insurance bill is due; you just don't think about it until it's in front of you. And it always lands at a bad time.

We call these your "true expenses" because they capture every expense involved in keeping your life running. When coming up with this list, think beyond scheduled bills to include expenses like car and home maintenance, or doctor visits. These are usually the expenses that convince people budgeting won't work for them. They think, "How can I budget for something when I don't know how much it will cost, or when it will happen?!" True, you won't know the particulars, but you do know that these costs *will* come up—and you know they'll cost more than zero. Save more than zero each month and they won't feel like a crisis when they hit. So when your four-year-old falls and splits open his lip on a Sunday night, the $300 urgent care visit won't cut into money you'd set aside for your fall foliage trip. And—shudder—you won't have to throw it on a credit card with a promise to figure it out later. You've set aside money for medical bills as a core essential, even if they aren't a steady monthly expense. You're prepared.

Prioritizing Your Priorities

If you've never been able to confidently cover your obligations, getting to this point is going to feel great. But you've just begun. Once your essentials are covered you can start thinking about your top priorities. You're still asking: *What do I want my money to do for me?* Only now you're out of survival mode and setting goals to design the life you want to live.

Don't worry if you don't have money left after funding your obligations. This is actually a good thing in many ways. To start, your money is no longer a black box. You have a sense of whether you're living within your means, and you can make informed spending decisions accordingly. Your answer to *Can I afford this?* won't be such a mystery, even if you may not like the answer. You'll be tempted to revert back to blissful ignorance, but hang in there. You're making progress just by knowing where you stand, and budgeting will get you closer to where you want to be.

Write down your quality-of-life goals even if you don't have money to assign to them right now. You will soon, and the moment you do you can put those dollars to work in exactly the way you want to.

Remember: You can do *whatever you want* with your money after your obligations are funded. Whatever you want! No pressure, right? It's funny how we can have no problem spending on a whim, but the idea of hashing out a meaningful plan for our money can be paralyzing. If we're super-busy we're quick to order takeout. If Anthropologie is having a sale we think we'd be crazy not to buy that $100 shirt for $30. Deciding whether to pay off our credit card or stash an emergency fund? Cue deer-in-headlights mode.

This won't be the case for everyone, but it's not unusual to get stuck trying to figure out big-picture priorities. If you're feeling lost, take a hint from your emotions. How does paying for certain things—or not paying for them—make you feel? Don't worry, I'm not going to make you lie on the therapist's couch and "talk about your feelings." But it's worth paying attention to your emotional reactions to money. They can be a big indicator of your priorities.

For Lia and Adam, paying off their wedding debt felt so pressing that it made their list of "obligations." Practically speaking, they're right—they are literally obligated to pay their minimum balance to the credit card company every month. But more important to them, looking at that $10,000 balance made Lia's throat close up a little. It kept Adam up at night wondering if they'd be able to pay off the debt before their first child arrived. In hindsight they wish they'd opted for a more frugal wedding, but they were young and excited (a whole year younger than when they started budgeting!), and they'd gotten swept away by the lure of limousines and an oyster bar. They loved their wedding but the fallout of that lingering bill is literally making them sick. Paying it off is a nonnegotiable priority for them.

Obvious stressors like Lia and Adam's wedding debt are no-brainers, and if you carry consumer debt, you may be feeling the same way. I have a lot to say about debt in the pages ahead, but for now just think about it in terms of your emotions. Picture how you'd feel if you threw a big chunk of money at your debt each month. Would it feel like an accomplishment? Like you're chipping away at removing a weight from your shoulders? Or would you feel stressed about other things you might not be accomplishing because your debt is eating most of your paycheck?

Maybe you hate your debt, but you also hate the idea of waiting to save a little for your kid's college until your debt is paid off. That inner conflict can reveal your answer: put a little toward both. I personally don't believe in saving for college (more on that later) and I can't stand debt—not even if it's my own mortgage—so I make it a priority to pay down any balances at a ferocious pace. Neither approach is right or wrong. Pick the one that brings you the most peace.

Also remember that budgeting isn't just about tackling your burdens. The bigger goal is to help you move toward living the life you want, so also give priority to the things that bring you joy and peace of mind. What would make you feel you're living a full, happy life? Do you want to travel? Spend time with family? Spruce up your home? Or maybe your idea of peace and happiness is just knowing you can go out to dinner once a week, guilt-free. Take the time to think about what makes you happy and **add those things to your budget**—even if they're just ambitious notes right now, with no dollars yet available for them.

Priority Hack

Here's a likely scenario: you've funded your obligations and are happy to see a few extra bucks in your bank account. (If you haven't hit this point, you will after a few months of budgeting.)

Sweet! You can finally start putting money toward the things you want to do. And there's so much you want to do. Maybe you've been dying to replace that old backyard fence and put up a swing set. You'd love for your yard to be a nice play area for your kids and their friends. But you've also been meaning to take them on a trip. You adore your small town but you want to make sure your kids know there's a whole world out there to be discovered.

What to do?

Should you spend on sprucing up the yard, or go on the trip?

Can you afford either of these things? Maybe that "extra" money isn't actually extra because you should be putting it toward your retirement or some other smart thing you're probably forgetting.

Sometimes just figuring out your priorities can be overwhelming, especially if you're new to this. The good news is that there's no wrong answer—but you still need to decide.

If you're struggling between a few options, stop to do some

deep prioritizing. What's more important to you? Experiences? Take the vacation. Solidity? Upgrade the yard. Inflating those savings accounts? Put some dollars aside.

Maybe you're still shrugging your shoulders. It can be difficult to separate yourself from the here-and-now. So try this: Imagine your future self having done each thing on your list. Which feels better? Seeing the kids and their friends enjoying the yard? Bike riding through Amsterdam as a family? The sense of security knowing you're helping with college? Or imagine your future self explaining to a good friend why you chose one over the other. Does it feel right?

If you're still not sure, enjoy the fact that this is a good problem to have. And know that this will get easier. Budgeting— and prioritizing—is like a muscle you exercise. The more you do it, the better you'll be at it.

You'll also begin to impress yourself by your ability to save and spend wisely so you can get what you want, sooner. What once seemed like a black-and-white decision becomes a riddle to solve. If your deep priority check reveals that a fat college savings account, an enjoyable yard, *and* family travel are equally important to you, you'll find a way to make each one happen—perhaps sooner than you even thought. Maybe you get a DIY swing set, or even spruce up a used one from Craigslist, and get wise on travel hacking strategies to book a cheaper trip. The extra funds go right to college.

The best part is that this won't be the last time you have extra money. The more you budget, the more you'll find yourself with extra money on hand. And you'll get better and better at knowing what you want it to do for you.

DEALING WITH DEBT

I have so much to say about debt, and yet, so very little. I can sum up everything you need to know about it in four words: *Get rid of it.*

I'm talking mostly about consumer debt, and here's why: Once you start budgeting and getting laser-focused on your priorities, you're making real progress toward your present and future goals. You've pinpointed the things that are most important to you and you're making a plan to get them. That's awesome!

But wait. If you have debt, a chunk of your dollars is already spoken for. That means your debt is literally stealing from your ability to fund your current priorities.

What stinks is that, for most of us, consumer debt is the result of a bunch of purchases we didn't really care about. That's not true for everything—sometimes life got in the way, or there was a medical emergency or some other unavoidable and necessary expense that got us into debt. But a lot of the time, that credit card balance is the fallout from buying things that didn't mean much to us. It's an accumulation of lunches we don't remember, new shirts we didn't wear, and trips to see movies we didn't even like. And it's keeping us from reaching the goals we've set for ourselves today.

Now, like everything in your budget, your priorities will influence the rate at which you pay off your debt. If you don't mind chipping away at it slowly (*really* slowly) you could just pay the minimum balances—those are nonnegotiable obligations—and carry on. I despise having debt, so I get intense—okay, obsessive—about paying off any balances as soon as I can.

I'm not going to tell you to go crazy paying off your consumer debt. It's really up to you (if those wild interest rates don't light a fire under you, nothing I say will). But remember that the more you're on the hook for past decisions, the less you'll be able to put toward today's priorities. The only way to put the past behind you is by killing those balances.

You're the Only One Who Can Make These Decisions

This is the point in most personal finance books where the author tells you what to do with your money: Pay down your credit cards with the highest interest rates first. Invest in this kind of index fund. Save for retirement no matter what. Don't go on vacation until you're out of debt.

A lot of people ask me to tell them what to do. Who can blame them? Life would be much easier with an instruction manual, it's true, but I can't do it. There are parts of this that you just have to figure out on your own. Okay, I did go on a little rant about paying down debt just a page ago, but that's as far as I'll go. You're the only one who can know what's right for you depending on your priorities and situation. I promise that once you do some inner digging, the decisions you make on your own will be so much more powerful than any step-by-step instructions I could give you. That makes the plan a new breed and easier to stick to.

I'm especially wary of financial advice based on percentages: housing should be X% of your income, food Y%, retirement Z%. Geography alone makes most of these generalities useless (hello, Iowa versus San Francisco rent). They're also blind to so many connected life choices. Maybe you spend more than the "recommended percentage" on rent, but you also don't own a car and you bike to work. Boom: car insurance, car payments, fuel, and gym memberships have no place in your budget. This is just one way that cookie-cutter advice rarely works.

Sure, I'll always tell you to fund your obligations first. I have big opinions about things like debt. And the Four Rules are universal to any financial situation. But they won't tell you exactly what to do with 20% of your paycheck a week from next Wednesday. The details are up to you and what you want your life to look like.

After lining up their obligations, including vanishing that wedding debt as soon as possible, Lia and Adam decided on these as their top priorities:

Travel: Lia is from New York and Adam is from Australia. They met on the road and always knew travel would be a big part of their life together. At a minimum, they decided to fiercely protect $3,000 each year to visit Adam's family in Melbourne. He's close with his parents and siblings and the thought of not having a home visit to look forward to makes him miserable. Family is also a top priority to Lia and she relies on those visits to build her relationships with her in-laws.

They hope to stash away more so they can visit a new country every year, but the high emotions surrounding the Melbourne trip make it nonnegotiable.

Health/Exercise: This includes gym memberships, funds for Adam to purchase new running shoes every few months, and other fitness-related expenses. They decided this spending is nonnegotiable since they take their wellness seriously. Adam is also training for a marathon, which they both agreed is an important goal worth funding.

What about Emergency Funds? Talk of budgeting often ends up in talk of emergency funds—but setting money aside is only half the battle. All your dollars need jobs. And Lia's peace of mind is linked to having enough money on hand to cover their expenses for six months if they were to lose their jobs. Adam is not as worried, but he knows Lia will be stressed without those savings. Most people would call this an "emergency fund" but we don't look at it that way at YNAB. Instead, it's a specific job for your money, just like this month's groceries or date nights. (We also see it as aging your money—yes, that's Rule Four—but I'll cover the idea in detail in Chapter 5.) For now, it's enough to know that Lia and Adam make it a top priority to funnel cash into funding *future months*, with the goal of having enough on hand for the next six months' worth of expenses.

House down payment: This goal makes the wedding debt especially hard to look at. Lia and Adam didn't realize how badly they wanted a house until the wedding was over and they started picturing day-to-day life with kids. Thankfully the rent on their one-bedroom apartment is below market value, so they feel good about that, but they're eager to have a porch and backyard before, well, before chaos and kids arrive.

Lia and Adam's budget also includes the following flexible goals. They tighten spending on these as needed until their higher priorities are covered:

Birthdays/Holidays: Lia and Adam stash away a little each month for gifts so they're prepared for special occasions (more on this strategy in the next chapter). Since this spending is highly adjustable, it's one of the first categories they skip if they don't have enough for high priorities.

Restaurants/Going out: This is a low priority. They care much more about funding their Melbourne trip and paying off wedding debt than they do about takeout sushi. They enjoy time out with friends but they'd rather surf or hike than go to a bar, so most of their fun is free. When priorities call they skip restaurants altogether and hit the trails for fun.

Fun money: They each get a few bucks to spend on themselves, no questions asked. I recommend this category to everyone (more about this on page 131). It gives you freedom to indulge in little things guilt-free while still staying within your budget.

Clothing: This is another category that they throw a couple hundred bucks into, then forget about until it's been depleted. If a top priority calls they can easily pull from Clothing, or any of these categories, to fund more important goals.

Lia and Adam are a long way from being debt-free globe-trotters, but now they can see the path in front of them. And it's a path that's one hundred percent tailored to their lifestyle and priorities. When they get stressed looking at their credit card balance they perk up knowing their Melbourne trip will be funded by June. Life isn't on total lockdown.

Other budgeting systems might tell them they're fools to spend on travel when their credit card balance is riding a 15% APR rate, or that they should forget the house until the debt is gone. You already know I'm obsessive about paying down debt, but I don't advocate sacrificing your (true!) happiness to get there. Lia and Adam probably wouldn't last long on a plan that pushes them to ignore the other priorities that, to them, make for a good life. You have to do what's right for you, today and long-term. It may be tempting to follow someone else's instructions, but they don't know a thing about you or your life. Trust yourself—you have what it takes to figure out what's best for you.

A New Way to Look at Your Credit Cards

You'll use Rule One for things you buy now even if you're putting them on a credit card. What's that? You thought paying your credit card bill itself was a Rule One job? There's more to it than that. If you have a big balance like Lia and Adam do, Rule One will have you assigning dollars to pay down the debt. But you'll also need to change your approach to new credit card purchases to avoid future debt. This is true for everyone who uses credit cards—whether you carry a balance or pay your bill in full.

Don't worry, I'm not going to tell you to kill your credit cards. I know most budgeting methods encourage you to slice up your plastic. They argue that with such high interest rates and the constant temptation to spend money you don't have, credit cards are the reason most of us are in financial trouble.

Fair enough, but I disagree. Credit cards are not the problem—it's how we use them. You're fine to use credit cards as long as you use them to spend the money that's already in your bank account. Money you've *already budgeted*. But hold on: this is not the same as having the money to pay your bill when it's due. Paying your bill is a great start, but if you only have enough to pay the *statement balance* when it's due there's a chance you're still spending more than you actually have.

At YNAB we talk a lot about what we call the Credit Card Float. If you're riding "the float" it means you're relying on next month's income to fund this month's spending. It can be hard to detect the float because most people who are trapped in this cycle are those who take pride in paying their credit card balance in full, every month, on time. They never pay interest and reap whatever rewards their credit card offers, whether it's miles, cash back, or a free pony. If you're one of these people, you're in better financial shape than most. But let's take a close look at how this setup usually works.

Let's say you charge a bunch of stuff on your credit card in October. The month's billing period closes on October 30 and the payment is due on November 30. Meanwhile, you continue charging stuff throughout November. The bill for that November spending won't be due until December.

Here's the test: When payment for your October spending is due on November 30, can you pay your card down to $0? In other words, can you pay for October's spending *and* whatever you spent in November? Or would you have to wait until you get paid in December to cover the difference?

If you don't have enough in the bank to pay your card down to $0, you're riding the Credit Card Float—and this isn't a fun amusement park kind of ride. This diagram helps explain it:

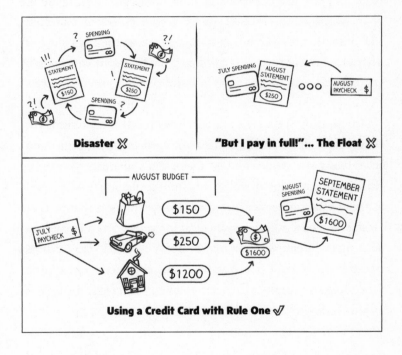

Disaster ✗   **"But I pay in full!"... The Float** ✗

Using a Credit Card with Rule One ✓

The Credit Card Float usually hovers without harm because you get your paycheck, pay the statement balance, and move on. But what if that next paycheck didn't come, for whatever reason? Or a major expense came up that ate into your check? Could you still pay your bill with the money you have on hand?

Whether you're riding the float or buried in credit card

debt, YNAB's strategy for using credit cards will keep you from spending money you don't have. The approach is simple: only charge something if that money is already in the bank and it's budgeted toward that expense. When you do this, you're using your credit card only because you *want* to (yay, points!), not because you *have* to (I can pay this bill as soon as my next check arrives!). You're essentially using it like a debit card. The only difference is that the cash stays in your checking account until you pay the bill. And you can pay the bill any day of the month, because the money is always there.

This approach also ensures that any credit card balances you might have don't *grow*. Your credit card payment will really have two parts: your debt paydown plus whatever you spent this month. It's the only way you can keep using credit cards without sinking deeper into debt. If you worry it will be confusing, you can use a separate card for your current spending. That one will get paid down to $0 every month. Also consider using cash or debit until your credit card balance is gone. Don't use any credit card that carries a balance—just focus on paying it down.

Bring in More Money, but Use It Wisely

It seems like a no-brainer that bringing in more money will ease your financial stress—especially if you're in debt—but this isn't a given. So much depends on how you handle that extra income. If you celebrate your raise by splurging (bigger apartment, hotter car, more HD channels, whatever), you'll be right where you were before. Perhaps even worse off.

Such is the curse of lifestyle creep. Perhaps you've heard the phrase before. Lifestyle creep is when the cost of your lifestyle rises in tandem with your income. Any income bump goes toward paying higher expenses. The common refrain (we've all probably said this at one point) is something along the lines of, "I'm actually making pretty good money now and I feel just as stressed with my money situation as ever."

Lifestyle creep is actually just a manifestation of your money not being lined up with your priorities. Yes, it all comes back to priorities. I actually think of it more as priority *seep* than lifestyle creep. If you're feeling discontent about your money, even after an income bump, it's likely because your money is not lining up with what's important to you.

So, how to combat lifestyle creep? Or, put another way, how do we make sure our money is consistently lining up with our priorities? I recommend two tactics that can be used together:

Question everything. Once a year (I like to do this in January), question every one of your expenses. Question the "givens" like housing, transportation, and insurance. Question the vacations you always take, the gifts you always buy, and the food you always eat. Every single item should be on the table. Following the tactic of asking *why* six or seven times as it relates to any one of your line items will help you peel back the layers of that priority and really see it for what it is.

This reminds me of my friend Sean. His family loved going to the movies. They loved the popcorn, the ambience, the movie, the smells, the time together as a family—maybe even the sticky floors? As Sean talked about these outings I could see that he truly loved them. This wasn't about knocking out a habit or convenience. So we peeled back that priority by asking *why* several times. Turns out, the core of what his family loved about these trips was the time they spent together. So I helped him strategize: Was there a way he could optimize the spending while maintaining or even improving that time together as a family? Yes.

Sean kept the movie night, but they did it at home. They still popped delicious popcorn, with that buttery smell traveling throughout the home, enjoyed a great movie, and spent time together. He said the family time actually improved. They would spend more time prepping and really making the movie night something special.

Between the movie tickets and expensive popcorn for a large family, they're ahead about $80 per movie night. The savings aren't the important part, though! Because they're now really dialed in to why movie night is important to them, they're doing things to maximize their time together. That's where it really counts.

So question everything. Even buttery popcorn.

Start fresh every year or two. I talk more about this in Chapter 9 but it's worth mentioning now. Sometimes you just need to burn down your budget. If you're using our software, you can do this using the "Fresh Start" feature we have built right in. If you're using a spreadsheet, file it away and start a new one. The idea is to start with just your bank account balance, then slowly add in your expenses one at a time. Where in the first tactic above you're asking what you could optimize or take away, with a fresh start you're asking what you should include. When you start with no expenses, each one must pass your scrutiny before even being allowed in. It's a twist from above, but it has one interesting effect. Usually when fairly experienced budgeters do this they have a big pile of money simply because they've been budgeting for so long. They all report that seeing the money in their checking account and having to allocate it to their priorities makes them feel those larger amounts a bit more. The exercise leads them to question their spending on a deeper level.

It's tempting to use a raise as an opportunity to upgrade your lifestyle, and if that's truly what you want, go for it. Just be careful about defaulting to new spending just because the money is suddenly there. Make sure your priorities are always driving your decisions.

YNAB'S PRIORITY CHEAT SHEET

Knowing what to prioritize first doesn't always come naturally, so at YNAB, we encourage following this clear Rule One hierarchy:

• Take care of your **immediate obligations** first—a roof over your head, food for you and your family, and bills like electric and heat that mean bad things if you don't pay them. Just setting aside money for these and knowing it's there will help you be more secure and *feel* more secure.

• Then move to the **true expenses** (more about these in Chapter 3). These are large, irregular expenses that surprise you (you know the feeling) but really shouldn't.

• Now the real fun kicks in. What are your **highest priorities** after your obligations? Family time? A hobby that borders on obsession? I won't judge, but fund those next.

• From there, we get into things that require money, but are **just for fun**. The sky wouldn't fall if they didn't get funded for a month.

The choices are still yours, but following this structure can help you learn what's important to you, and what might just have been spending habits you'd happily drop.

CHAPTER 3:

Rule Two—Embrace Your True Expenses

You've already met Rule Two: Embrace Your True Expenses. You know it prompts you to break down big expenses by assigning dollars to them each month. Enough said, right?

Sort of. Here's the thing about Rule Two: it has the power to completely transform your money situation. I know that sounds a little like infomercial-speak, but stay with me (because it's not).

Rule Two is all about thinking long, and acting now. It lets you get a grip on what's coming so you're not stuck holding an empty bag when you need money later. *What's coming* can be anything from a bill to a big life goal. Think long, act now, and you'll have the money for all of it.

I introduced the idea of your "true expenses" in the last chapter—the idea that it isn't just the regular, monthly expenses that you need to keep your life running. When I talk about Rule

Two, I'm specifically focusing on the infrequent expenses that tend to sneak up on us, but to be clear, your true expenses are *ALL of your expenses*—the daily, the monthly, and the irregular ones that we often forget. The concept of "true expenses" helps us see that what we usually think of as our expenses don't capture the full picture.

Most of your dealings with Rule Two will involve your infrequent expenses, and they generally fall into two camps: **Predictable**, and **Unpredictable but Inevitable.**

Your **predictable** expenses are, well, predictable. Although they take many people by surprise, we all know exactly when they're due and how much they'll cost. Or at least, we all have access to this information if we bother to pay attention. Car insurance premiums are one of the biggest offenders here. You know the feeling when that huge bill hits your mailbox. It's always the last thing you expect, and it feels like you just paid it . . . oh, wait . . . six months ago. You often have no choice but to throw it on a credit card, or reluctantly write a check using money you'd hoped to spend on something else.

Now imagine how you'd feel on the day your $600 insurance premium is due if you'd saved $100 a month over the last six months. You wouldn't flinch. There would be no stress around it at all. In fact, you'd probably feel pretty happy and proud that you can just pay your bill and move on. You'd remember the times when facing a bill like this was stressful—and that memory would make the good feeling even sweeter.

Other predictable expenses don't have a set amount, but we still know exactly when the spending will happen, so we can plan for it. You know your shopping will spike in December. You know the AC will bully your electric bill in summer and your gas or oil bill will soar in winter. You know you'll need a good chunk of money to fly the family to Grandma's for Thanksgiving. And you know the postholiday dread that comes with your bloated credit card statement. It's always stressful.

It may sound crazy to start saving for holiday shopping in February, but think how you'll feel when that lump of cash is just sitting there in December, waiting for you to spend it guilt- and stress-free. The same goes for any bills that jump at certain times of the year. Future You will be so happy with Past You for thinking ahead and putting a little aside all year.

Your **unpredictable but inevitable** expenses, on the other hand, are the things you know you'll need to spend money on at some point—you just don't know when or exactly how much. These are a little more of a wild card compared to your predictable expenses, but they're not as erratic as we tend to believe.

Think back to any time you've looked at your credit card statement and decided that your huge balance was just because of "an especially crazy month." Maybe your surprise charges looked something like this: A gift for the wedding you attended, that GoFundMe donation for your coworker's daughter, a new tire after you drove too close to the curb to avoid that pothole (both came out of nowhere!), and—gah!—a last-minute suit for that wedding because your old one is two sizes too big (the only downside to hitting your weight loss goal). None of your spending was unreasonable or irresponsible. Some of it was even generous and kind! So you brush it off as an unusual month and promise next month will be better.

Next credit card statement: supplies for a science fair project, a copay for an x-ray after you tripped barefoot over a bike in the garage (don't go barefoot in the garage), printer ink so expensive it should be illegal, surprise surgery for the family cat. Another crazy month, but that's okay. Really and truly, next month will be better. Next month will be *regular*.

You know how this ends. It never gets better, because it's not an "especially crazy month." It's just life.

Those surprise expenses are what stop most people from budgeting. They feel it's impossible to plan for the unplanned, so why bother?

Here's the thing: many of your surprise expenses aren't surprises at all. Look at your life from a broader view. You know tires don't last forever (set something aside each month for auto maintenance). You know your fifteen-year-old cat is bound to have medical problems (fund your vet category when she's healthy, too). You know you're a softie for any fund-raising campaign in your Facebook feed that involves kids (treat yourself to a "giving" category). These charges aren't flare-ups in your spending. Yes, they're unexpected in the moment they hit, but they're inevitable, which means you know they'll surface at some point. They're true expenses—and you can plan for them.

Predictable or not, you can get a pretty strong hold on your true expenses just by looking at some past credit card statements. Maybe this will be painful for you, but it will be worth even a quick skim to pick up on important patterns like the frequency of your vet visits, charitable giving, or infrequent bills. It's also a great chance to reinforce your priorities. If you cringe with every pizza order you see, use that frustration as ammunition to align your spending with your goals moving forward. This isn't about dwelling on the past—you're just peering at it long enough to fully understand where your money is really going (and where you might want it to go instead).

Rule One Redux

I can't keep going without admitting something: Rule Two is actually Rule One. Each of the Four Rules is actually just Rule One for different scenarios. In this case, Rule Two is simply Rule One for less frequent expenses.

Once you've identified your true expenses, it all goes back to Rule One. With your immediate obligations funded, go down your priority list and assign dollars to jobs in order of importance. If you're not sure what to fund first, try targeting the infrequent bills that *always* tend to blindside you, or the spending peaks, like holidays, that always set you back. The ones that make you cringe when you even think of them. Then fund the others as you can.

Now, be warned: Rule Two has some side effects. For one thing, you're going to have more money. Since you're not spending on these jobs every month (although you are setting money aside each month), you literally end up with piles of money just sitting there, waiting to be spent. It's a beautiful thing.

You'll also quickly discover that the more you fund your infrequent expenses, the less stressed you'll feel. In fact, your money stress will disappear in direct proportion to the amount of money you set aside for your long-term spending targets—especially your top-priority areas, because it just feels so good to put money toward the things that are important to you. (I'm sure there's some very official science out there that proves this.)

Dream Big, Act Small

Another beautiful thing about Rule Two (there are so many beautiful things about it) is that it gives you a simple, concrete strategy for achieving big goals. Sure, it helps with expenses, but remember that budgeting is really about designing the life you want. Rule Two is your secret weapon for getting closer to that dream life.

When I opened this chapter I went on about how Rule Two can transform your money situation. It really can, as long as you don't underestimate its power to help you accomplish *huge* goals. Think about all of those things you'd like to achieve that seem so far-fetched. They feel more like fantasies than life goals. Your dreams don't have to be epic to be transformative. Again, maybe you just wish you didn't feel so stressed about money all the time. Rule Two is perfect for that. Think about how much stress stems from the "surprise" expenses that always make us feel we can't get ahead, or the big debts we dream of vanishing. If you take a broader view of your spending and stockpile money for those big expenses, that stress will disappear.

I often compare Rule Two to the idea of trying to climb a large mountain. It looks daunting—even impossible—but if you break it up into small hills, your heart rate barely registers the effort. Little ups and downs are so much easier to manage than big ones, whether you're scaling a mountain or working toward a financial goal. Ten thousand dollars in credit card debt can feel paralyzing. But break it up into a few hundred dollars a month and suddenly the difference between you and your dream of being debt-free is just fewer dinners out, one less pair of shoes, or a revised strategy at the grocery store each month. Every little victory inches you closer to your goal as you realize that it's the small decisions that add up to make a big difference.

Now, I understand there's probably a lot you want to do. It can be overwhelming to see everything on your money bucket list—from bills to goals—the first time you sit down with Rule Two. Remember to pace yourself, and give yourself a break. You're just starting to take control of your money. Don't expect to be able to fund everything. It takes a while to build up to being able to put something toward *every* goal every month, and maybe you don't even need to. Once you feel comfortable with a certain amount in a particular area (like maybe a vet or car-repair fund), you can stop filling it. That's easy.

Still, that full view of your true expenses can feel like a mountain to climb—or even a mountain range. With so many goals vying for your cash, it can be hard to know where to start. Put a little in each? Target one ferociously? This is where strategizing is so important. As I said earlier, start with the bills or expenses that always tend to knock you out when they arrive—insurance premiums, birthdays or holidays, big annual dues like summer camps or tuition. If you can fund one of these expenses just once before it's due, that momentum and good feeling will carry you through until you can gradually fund your other big expenses. And don't forget that the rest of your budgeting will also help you free up cash to make these true-expense targets achievable.

Also remember that your emotions are often a good measure of what you should tackle first, and that you have the power to be as tenacious as you want. Lia and Adam wanted to kill their wedding debt so badly, they dumped as much as they could into their bill each month. If you're feeling consumed by a goal, attack it as fiercely as it's attacking you—or not. Julie and I have goals in our budget that have no money in them at all. They're long-term targets that we'd like to accomplish one day, but they're not urgent enough to attract our dollars yet. Our big one right now is a family cabin. We'd love to save for one but we want to be mortgage-free before we start. So we put the cabin in our budget as a reminder, and something to look forward to.

Whatever your strategy, know that for every dollar to which you assign a job, you're a dollar better off than you were before. Do it again. Do it again. Do it again. Before you know it, you will have scaled that mountain without having stopped even once to catch your breath.

This Is Your Brain on Rule Two

Rule Two gets you to be proactive with your money on a much deeper level than you've ever experienced. When you think long and act now, you're not just looking at your immediate bills—you're seeing the bigger picture and you're hyperaware of *all* your expenses. Your spending doesn't surprise you anymore when you have this kind of clarity. Your bank statements may look roughly the same (perhaps with less pizza, but maybe not), only now you see how they reflect your broader life picture. That sharper focus will also influence the short-term spending decisions that have a big effect on your long-term money goals.

Put simply, Rule Two takes over your brain. Don't worry—this is a good thing. The biggest change is in your spending behavior. When your long-term goals are on your radar, your bank account balance is no longer the deciding factor in whether or not to buy something. The question stops being *Can I afford this?* You can likely *afford* lots of things if you have the cash on hand, but that's not the point. You're now asking yourself, "Does this move me closer to my goal(s)?" You're considering the future ramifications of your decision in a very concrete way, and spending becomes about real trade-offs: "If I buy these shoes now, it will take me an extra month to hit my vacation goal." You'll quickly find that, when looking at your spending through this lens, you make great decisions!

We already make trade-offs all the time, although we may not notice it because the trade-off tends to be vague and pretty useless. We think, "If I buy this, I'll have less money. Am I okay with that?" Well, how can you know if you're okay with it if you don't have a real sense of what the difference really means to you? Our motivation never lasts when we decide not to spend because we want more money. We'll always want more money—it's an unattainable goal. We end up feeling deprived because we're reining ourselves in by dangling an unreachable carrot.

Rule Two draws the line to real consequences. Now you're thinking, "If I buy this, I'll have less money *for that thing I want in three months.*" That reality makes all the difference. Now the trade-off isn't about having less money, it's about not having something you've decided you want. There's no deprivation there at all. You're *getting* something for your sacrifice. Something you actually want!

When this line of thinking becomes your new normal, magic happens. Money is found (by not being spent) and you start reaching your goals. The only change is that you're now proactively working on making progress toward whatever it is you want, whether that is a down payment on a house or a decent vet fund so you're prepared when the cat starts walking into walls. Every time you choose to put money toward a long-term priority, you're literally sending money ahead to the future, setting Future You up for success.

SEEING IS BELIEVING

Matthew Ricci is a twenty-nine-year-old client services manager living in New York City with his fiancée, Allie. He started using YNAB two years ago to get out of debt (which he did!). These days his top priorities are maxing out his retirement accounts and stockpiling cash for what he calls "bigger risks," like launching his own business.

Recently Matt and Allie started a shared budget to help them work as a team in combining their lives. Matt still has his personal budget—they plan to join their accounts once they're married—and the shared budget is for the expenses they split now: rent, groceries, eating out, and travel. They'd both tried several different ways of organizing their money in the past and were disappointed with the results, so Allie was skeptical that YNAB would work. But she rolled with it because Matt was such a Four Rules die-hard. (He once forwarded one of our emails about Rule Four to twenty-three of his friends, and you can't spend more than ten minutes with this guy without hearing about his budget. It happens, and I love him for it.)

Matt was excited about their shared budget and he hoped his enthusiasm would be contagious. When an invitation to a destination wedding hit their mailbox, he saw his chance to show Allie just how valuable the YNAB method could be. The wedding was six months away. Matt estimated that the trip would cost $1,000, which he broke into six installments that they passively funneled into their budget each month.

Six months later, Allie and Matt were sipping umbrella drinks at their friends' nuptials. They'd accumulated the full cost of the trip in their budget and the cash was just waiting to be spent.

"I definitely watched the 'click' happen in Allie's eyes," Matt says. "She was amazed that the $1,000 was painlessly there. It was a big moment."

Allie may never be as intense about YNAB as Matt is, but she's seen the power of Rule Two in action, and she's in.

Rule Two Nirvana: No More Emergency Funds

I'll say it again: there are so many beautiful things about Rule Two. One of my favorites is the fact that, once you're really rolling with it, the idea of an "emergency fund" becomes obsolete. I know that nearly every financial guru tells us we need to have a certain number of months' worth of expenses stashed away in a big untouchable lump. But the money you set aside for Rule Two *is your emergency fund.* Only better, it's more targeted, more proactive, and likely to have you better prepared than that vague bubble of money sitting in the bank without a specific purpose.

Put another way, when you implement Rule Two, fewer things feel like "emergencies" because you've already planned for them (at least financially). Don't get me wrong—there will always be a place for the "I lost my job" emergency fund. It's smart to be prepared if your income stream suddenly dries up. But even in that case, we don't recommend having the money just sit there in a generic pile labeled "emergency." Instead, assign the cash you have to future expenses. If you have eight months' worth of "emergency fund" on hand, budget out your true expenses for the next eight months (remember, true expenses are *all your expenses*—the daily, the monthly, and the infrequent). If you're working toward building those reserves, assign your cash to jobs in future months as it comes in. Or, if you're just worried about income loss and have saved money to cover that, call it what it is. Think of it as an income replacement fund and then you'll never touch it for an impulse splurge. The *really important job* you gave that money—different from a generic emergency fund—protects your original intention. Technically your bank account will look the same as if that money were a generic emergency fund—it will just sit there as one big sum. But your budget will tell the full story: you'll know exactly what each dollar will cover, and for how long.

Again, this is what Rule Four: Age Your Money is all about. I'll take a deep dive into this topic later, but I can't talk about Rule Two's emergency fund takeover without a Rule Four spoiler. The bottom line is, if your true expenses are well funded, your job crisis will be much less of a crisis because you won't be living paycheck to paycheck.

Rule Two funds are also much less likely to get raided, since we're holding them with a purpose. We can easily rationalize plucking money from a generic emergency fund when we're not sure exactly what it's being held for. But when you know that money is for medical bills, you're much less likely to siphon from it to pay for a birthday present. And if you do take the money (okay, you're healthy today and your mom will be really disappointed if you skip her birthday), you know how much you need to put back, and why. The stakes are clear.

Calling All Workers with a Variable Income

Rule Two tends to scare away would-be budgeters who don't earn a steady paycheck. I've worked with hundreds of people who fall into this camp: freelancers, waitstaff, consultants, or anyone working on commission.

People with a variable income often tell me their situation is just too unique for a cookie-cutter budget. A budget, with all its long-term goals pining for dollars, seems way too rigid when your income trickles and flows at an erratic pace. A budget feels so set in stone, so contrary to reality, that freelancers and *anyone* whose income changes from month to month avoid budgeting altogether—or quit the moment cash flow picks up or dries out. If you've gotten this far in the book, you know that a budget is meant to be flexible. But from a distance, it can seem like a stifling box when your cash flow is so irregular.

But all of that is a huge misconception. In truth, if you're living on a variable income, you need a budget more than anyone. That's not because you're bad with money—it's because there's so much more room for error when your cash flow is not predictable. Without fail, a client's payment will be late in the month a big bill is due. An infrequent expense will hit and wipe out your bank account on a low-cash-flow month. A project will be delayed. That trip you'd planned so meticulously will cost more than expected. Common money surprises hit so much harder when you don't have that regular paycheck on which to fall back. These are the moments when your budget will save you.

The other, often hidden, risk when your income is variable is that it's easier to trick yourself into feeling rich on the months when a big payment lands. Those are the times you exhale and think, "Things are great. What was I ever worried about?" It's tempting to avoid important money decisions and blow your chance at stabilizing your cash flow on the high-income months, when you feel everything is going so well that you've earned yourself a new pair of boots.

This is all normal—life on a variable income is usually lived in one extreme or another: panic in low-income months, euphoria in high-income months. It's a wild seesaw ride (which you've chosen because it happens to come with what you're passionate about in your career) that rarely gives you time to look at your finances with clarity. That's why a budget is so important. It's a tool that helps you to be consistent with your money when your income is anything but.

The fact that a budget is monthly sometimes trips up people who get paid at different intervals. They feel it just doesn't apply to them, but looking at your expenses month-to-month is actually a great framework for keeping your goals and obligations organized. It lets you plan for the common monthly expenses and pace yourself as you work toward bigger goals. Looking at your expenses by month will also give you a clear view of where you stand financially. You may feel rich when that five-figure payment lands, but plugging it into your monthly budget will show you the real picture.

Maybe you *are* rolling in it, and you don't have to worry about money for the next six months. That's great, especially if you're factoring in infrequent big bills for the foreseeable future. Just make sure that "extra" $1,000 is truly extra before spending it on a cruise when your tuition bill is due in two months and your next check won't arrive until well after that. You may not like the truth, but you'll be better off.

Budgeting forces you to make decisions you'd otherwise avoid when you think you're steeped in cash. You *need* this clarity on a variable income, or else the agony of your low-income months will be so much worse than the joy that comes with big payments. Your money may be a wild roller coaster, but your feelings around your money don't have to be. Budgeting keeps the vibe at a steady stream of "feeling okay," until "feeling pretty happy" becomes the new normal.

The Great College Debate

Speaking of long-term financial goals, here's one that's not on my list: saving for college. I have six kids, and not one of them has a college fund. Seriously.

I know I'm not the only parent who is purposely *not* saving for college. My friend and fellow YNAB team member Todd is another nonsaver, and we each do it for different reasons. In my family's case, I plan to help my kids get through college debt-free not by stockpiling cash that will cover the tab, but by teaching them to fund their tuition via a blend of scholarships, budgeting, and working while in school. I'm hugely averse to student loans, so they're not part of the plan, either. One reason is that I hate debt (as you know), but I also think it's a scam that young people with very little understanding of money are made to believe taking on five- and sometimes six-figure loans is the only way to get a good education. It's not true, and it robs them of a solid decade of having complete control over their money after college.

The best thing we can do for our kids is to help them see that student debt is not the only option (I say debt is *never* an option!). Working while in school and applying for scholarships are a good start. Also help them see that fancy schools with high price tags are not always worth the costs. Too many factors go into choosing a college for me to really get into it here. The bottom line is that your kids have choices beyond student loans. Make sure they know that.

I also stand behind Todd's reason for not saving for college, which is that he and his wife, Jessica, would rather put the money toward shared experiences with their family now. This year they spent a sizable chunk of money for their family of five to live in France for five weeks. Their kids were nine, eleven, and thirteen years old at the time, and they'd calculated that if they'd instead put that money toward college, it *might* have covered one child's tuition for one semester. Those numbers aren't bad. I do tout the benefits of saving in small increments (think long and act now, right?), but the decision goes back to trade-offs. When faced with the choice to either save a small percentage on future tuition or have a life-changing family experience, Todd and Jessica will choose the adventure today every time.

And it isn't just about adventure or dollar-for-dollar trade-offs that only an accountant could love—those experiences are worth something to Todd and Jessica. Plus, what if two of their kids get scholarships while the other decides he wants to start a business instead of going to college right away? They would have missed out on the life experiences that Todd and his family feel are so important. So while she doesn't have a lump of college savings in her name, Todd's daughter Sadie got to visit a boulangerie every day and buy bread for her family, on her own, in a language she'd been learning for just a few months. The whole family got the daily opportunity to be in different surroundings, with different foods, different ways of living and getting around, and different expectations. They got to see that the world isn't the same as their small town in Massachusetts. The family couldn't have had that experience *and* put thousands in a college fund that summer. So they happily chose their one priority for that money.

One can make so many logical arguments against this thinking, but it's what Todd and Jessica want for their family—and their money.

Nobody's pithy advice, not even mine, is going to help you through these big decisions. The Four Rules will give you a structure for thinking through your options, but the choices themselves are all yours.

RULE TWO:
EMBRACE YOUR TRUE EXPENSES

Most of us aren't used to thinking of spending in terms of true expenses, but once you embrace this mindset you'll start to feel the power of financial freedom. Hardly any bill or spending jump will be a surprise—and you'll have the money, just sitting there.

Remember, your true expenses fall into two groups:

• **Predictable** expenses aren't frequent but we know exactly when they'll hit and how much they'll cost. There are bills like insurance premiums and car registrations, but also remember predictable spending bumps: holiday shopping, summer camp, gardening supplies, back-to-school clothes. Even if they're not set amounts, you can set spending goals and break them into monthly targets that you fund throughout the year.

• **Unpredictable but inevitable** expenses are things like car repairs, impulse donations, wedding gifts, shampooing the carpets after your aging dog forgets to go outside for certain activities . . .

Rule Two is also your superpower for life goals. Want to start a business, buy a motorcycle, backpack through Africa, or do *whatever*, to you, makes for a good life? Set a goal, break it down into manageable monthly amounts, and start funding the life you want.

CHAPTER 4:

Rule Three—Roll with the Punches

Here's an experiment: Write a plan right now for exactly what you're going to do next Friday, down to the hour. When next Friday comes, let me know how closely you stuck to your plan.

We don't have to wait until Friday to know how this will go. You'll make changes. You'll have every good intention of doing certain things, like picking up your dry cleaning, but you'll get held up helping your neighbor carry a futon down three flights of stairs. You'll do laundry rather than working in the garden since it's raining. Even if your plan involves going to work, a vortex of email and meetings might derail your schedule (what time did you say you were going to leave?). Anything can and will happen, because there's a difference between a plan and real life.

Does this mean you shouldn't plan? No, and in fact the gap

between your *actual* day and your *planned* day will depend on how you approach the plan.

There's the no-plan approach to planning, where you're just working off of fleeting thoughts. Slim chance you'll achieve much with that. The same goes if you write the plan and then forget about it. You'll spend next Friday doing who-knows-what, and by nightfall you'll have wondered where the day went. Whatever you do will have happened on a whim, with little regard for what you'd actually hoped to accomplish.

At the other extreme, if you obsess over sticking to the plan, down to the minute, despite any consequences, you're sure to be stressed and unhappy. Even if you don't mind policing your time so closely for one day, you will quickly burn out. And you probably still won't accomplish everything. Something will always come up. . . .

. . . You'll knock a mug on the ground as you're walking out the door (you can't leave it to deal with later because the cat will get into the broken pieces).

. . . You'll get sucked into texting with your sister at work (seriously need to work on detaching yourself from your phone).

. . . Your best friend will call, ecstatic about the long-awaited promotion he just received, and can you meet him in thirty minutes to celebrate over lunch (but lunch was for going to the gym!)?

You get this. You know it's not realistic to micromanage your time. You understand your day won't go exactly as expected, and (depending on how type-A you are) you're fine with that. You also know you're more likely to accomplish your goals if you have *some kind* of plan, even if it ends up changing.

This is exactly how we should treat our budget: like a flexible plan.

The problem is, most people have a hard time seeing their budget as a living, adaptable thing. They feel that if they change it, they're not really budgeting, they're cheating—but that couldn't be more wrong.

Rule Three: Roll with the Punches is all about adjusting your budget to allow for whatever comes your way. Because your budget is a plan that reflects your life, and like life, plans (and budgets) change.

Let me say this again: it's okay to change your budget.

Scratch that (change, right?). You *have* to change your budget if you ever expect to stick with it.

Let me be clear here: I'm going right after that new mindset I want you to have. Change is so important that we've dedicated an entire rule to it. This isn't overkill—it's actually one of the biggest reasons people thrive on YNAB even if they've struggled with budgeting before. Rule Three is what will save you when all other budgeting apps, experts, and programs make you feel that you've failed the moment you stray from the original plan. It's what pulls your budget out of a spreadsheet and into the real world.

Accountability IRL

It's not your fault if changing your budget feels like failing. So much of the advice we hear about becoming financially successful revolves around this idea of self-discipline. Buck up and make your coffee at home. Shop "in your closet." Stop eating out. Any budget changes you make can feel like your self-discipline score is being docked another point. We're led to believe we won't ever succeed if we can't be accountable to our budget.

Accountability is critical, but let's be clear on what *accountability* actually is. Accountability is dealing with the truth of every decision you make. You're actually never more accountable than when you change your budget. (Go ahead, read that sentence again, it's important.) If you've overspent on eating out and need to take that money from a different priority, like vacation, that's accountability. You are living the reality of what it means to spend more than you'd planned: you're now that much farther from your vacation goal. It's not a failure, but a reprioritization.

You're not accountable to every line item in your budget. That would be like holding yourself to that hour-by-hour schedule you wrote a week ago. It just won't match reality. But you *are* accountable to your bottom line—that is, the balance between your money in versus money out. You can and should shift money between priorities when life demands (or requests!) it, but at the bottom line you know you have a finite amount of money. If you spend more than planned in one place, you have to pull that money from another spending goal because it doesn't exist anywhere else (and because debt is not an option!).

That big-picture thinking will keep you budgeting and moving closer to your goals. Sure, maybe you won't save $500 for vacation this month as planned, just like you probably won't pick up your dry cleaning at exactly 3 p.m. But setting those intentions may help you save $300 this month—money that would have gone to Chinese food and iTunes (neither of which you care about as much) if you hadn't been careful to set a plan in the first place. Likewise, if you hadn't planned to pick up your dry cleaning, your blazer would still be hanging from that revolving rack. The goals are what matter. As long as you keep moving toward them, you're succeeding.

It's normal for anyone dedicated to achieving a big goal to adjust their plan as they go. Think of the basketball coach making halftime adjustments, or a chess grandmaster adapting her approach as she sees how her opponent is defending. Or, for you gamers out there, when you're playing World of Warcraft and your raid can't down the boss so you three-heal instead of two-heal? (Nongamers, just gloss over that one, trust me.) It would be ludicrous for us not to expect adaptation from high-level operators in any situation, but when it comes to adapting our budget to new information, we're quick to label that a failure.

HOW DOLLARS ARE LIKE MINUTES, HOW MINUTES ARE LIKE DOLLARS

Still worried that changing your budget is cheating? Here's another way to think of it like time: You've got three hours before a deadline for a project at work, and a list of seven final tasks to complete on the project. There are no extensions. That's your bottom line, those finite three hours. So you make a plan and start checking off those last seven pieces. Suddenly, one of them takes much longer than you expected. So you adjust. You can't create more time, so you decide to nix two of the seven. You get the rest done and deliver the project (your client is thrilled, by the way; it turns out those two you cut were fluff you didn't need). You stay within the bottom-line accountability of your deadline.

That's how your budget works. You work only with the money you already have, and that's your bottom line. Shifting it around when life (or a client's project) calls for it is just smart.

Be Honest with Yourself

Along with freedom, Rule Three brings a healthy dose of honesty to your budget. By all means, change your budget when you need to, but also be aware of any patterns you're setting. If you're constantly adjusting to compensate for overspending in one area, you're probably not being honest with yourself when you budget that number in the first place.

If you're habitually adjusting your budget, it's like having that item on your today to-do list for a month. You know you're not going to declutter your closet today, or even this week, so either pull it off the list or reevaluate your priorities. Otherwise that task will just sit there, heckling you and making you feel like you're constantly underachieving.

Perhaps you'd love to spend $400 a month on groceries for your family of five, but if you overspend every month, $400 just isn't your reality right now. It could mean you simply have to budget more for groceries to meet your family's needs. Or if you're determined to make $400 work, you need to revamp your grocery game. Or if you decide to eat organic and local, you may suddenly have to do more than revamp—but that would be because you made that choice.

Julie and I overspent on groceries pretty much every month for a decade. I'm not kidding. Out of more than a hundred months we *maybe* hit our grocery goal ten times. We'd always set our food target with that first-of-the-month optimism that *this time* would be different. I, in particular, swore we just needed a few more coupons, or another look at the sale circulars, and we'd hit our goal. I knew Julie could do it, because this was Julie's domain. We'd both learned to be super-frugal when we were newlyweds but nobody could top Julie's ability to stretch our grocery dollars in those days.

Our grocery targets were based on our early spending patterns plus a little more as kids showed up. The numbers had worked for years. I just couldn't understand why we *never* hit our goal anymore.

Then, one night during a budget meeting, we finally peeled back the onion layers enough to reveal the truth: Julie was done being a price-slaying grocery diva. She'd hustled to stretch our dollars when we were broke and childless, but she didn't want to debate over pennies or optimize the food budget anymore. These days, it felt like a victory just to get the shopping done with the kids in tow without mayhem erupting. As she put it, "I do not care what a can of corn costs." Her priority was to just have a peaceful grocery experience.

I finally got it. It only took us ten years to uncover the truth, and that's probably because I was being lame for nine of those years, but we figured it out. We weren't in the tight financial spot that we'd been in when we first got married. We had the money to up our grocery spending and it was important to Julie to have that breathing room.

Just being honest that a change needs to happen can be so liberating. As soon as we started putting way more money into the grocery category, the tension was gone. We still wield Rule Three all the time—only now it's for actual surprises, not things we swear we'll do but know will never happen.

Life, Values, and Priorities

Rolling with the punches isn't always about adjusting your dollars when you overspend. Sometimes life just blindsides us, and we need to rejig our money plan just to keep up.

I'm talking about the flooded basement. The coffee spill on your new laptop. The sister who calls to say she's fifteen minutes away, and can she stay at your house for the next two weeks and eat all your food?

You'll have funds to cover surprises the longer you practice Rule Two, but sometimes the hits are so huge, and so unexpected, they completely derail your plans. That's when you'll start squeezing dollars out of every category that can spare them, and maybe feel weepy about all the money you're spending on something that wasn't even on your priority list.

But here's the thing about those big punches: perhaps they weren't on your priority radar, but they usually do reflect your values, which are your budget's driving force. While your priorities can actually change fairly quickly, your values are much more resilient. Sometimes we don't even notice our values are guiding us. We just get the feeling that a certain decision is "the right thing to do," or simply nonnegotiable.

Your family may be more important to you than anything or anyone else, so your little sister's request for her family to stay with you while their house gets treated for mold is a no-brainer. You probably don't have a Rule Two category that covers spontaneous family stays, but your values make helping your sister a big priority. You'll find a way to wring dollars out of other categories. Your budget will suddenly look very different, and making it work will be hard, but the values that drive your new money plan will be the same as before.

Your values can influence even the most unassuming decisions. Todd's garage door recently broke. It got stuck in the down position. The day before it broke, replacing the garage door was not a priority for Todd's family at all. The day after? Darn close to number one in their budget. Again, the values they base their budget on—security, a good home, educational and travel opportunities, fitness and healthy eating—didn't change. But their budget did.

Your values will also help you decide how much you're

willing to bend when the punches land. They'll even determine the gravity of the blow. If a coffee spill fried your new MacBook Pro, it could be an expensive and unfortunate nuisance if the computer was for personal use. But what if you're a freelancer and you need it to do your job? In that case, *not* replacing it means you won't be able to contribute to your household income. Suddenly the decision is nonnegotiable. Maybe your next computer can be cheaper, but the bottom line is that you have to buy a new one because you value a secure life for your family. Priorities shifted. Values intact.

WHEN BIG GOALS MEET BIG PUNCHES

Tracy and Dan Kellermeyer have leveraged YNAB to hit some pretty big goals. They knocked out $50,000 in consumer debt and saved $25,000 to pay for their wedding in cash (more about those adventures on page 146).

Shortly after their wedding, they paused their debt payoff to focus on another milestone: building a comfortable emergency fund. But they weren't able to save for long. They were putting $2,000 into savings each month for six months when they were blindsided by the biggest punch of their short marriage. In May 2016, Tracy was laid off from her job—just seven months after she and Dan said, "I do."

"I was devastated," Tracy recalls. "It cut our income by forty percent, but Dan kept reassuring me we would be fine because we were prepared."

Not only were they prepared thanks to their emergency fund; they'd been so used to living below their means to reach their financial goals that they didn't even need to touch that cash. "We definitely had to roll with the punches by adjusting our spending after May. We also stopped putting money into our savings. That combo kept us from having to dip into our emergency fund, which was huge. You work so hard to build that up, you really don't want to spend it!"

Stopping those $2,000 transfers to savings was Dan and Tracy's biggest change. They also cut their personal spending money in half. From there, they cut a little in other categories, like clothing, entertainment, restaurants, and the dog budget, so they didn't feel a shocking difference in any one place. They also sold Tracy's car and reprioritized that money. Dan worked from home so they were fine sharing his car, especially since Tracy wasn't driving to work anymore. That meant their car insurance and gas spending were also cut in half. Tracy started shopping at secondhand stores when she absolutely needed clothing, and she borrowed dresses from her sister when she needed something to wear for special occasions (where she would normally purchase something new). They also took advantage of their points from credit cards and cashed those out for extra money.

Tracy and Dan's experience is a reminder that the longer you budget, the less the punches will hurt when they do land. Even the mega-clobbers. Rules One and Two will help you roll with the punches:

- Rule One gets you laser-focused on the top priorities that need your dollars.
- You may not have a job-loss fund, but if you've been rolling on Rule Two for a while you will likely have enough on hand to cover a good amount of your expenses.

If you haven't gotten far with any of the rules, don't worry. Do what's necessary to get through the punches and keep budgeting. Let the experience motivate you to reach your financial goals. You'll see that when the next punch lands (and it will), it doesn't hurt as bad. The rules will weave you a nice little safety net.

The Family That Budgets Together . . .

Meet the Dale tribe. Their money story spans so many points in this book, you'll be hearing about them a couple of times. Let's start with the $40,000 hospital visit. You know, the one they're paying for . . . out of pocket.

In January 2016, nine-year-old Aspen Dale was not herself. She'd lost ten pounds over a few weeks and constantly felt sick. After a trip to the emergency room, her parents, Jon and Amy, got the surprising news: Aspen had type 1 diabetes.

Their life took a radical turn after that night. Financially, they had new medical expenses that would be part of Aspen's life indefinitely. Their health-care coverage reimburses their spending but they're in a situation where they have to pay the bills up front. That means a huge demand on their cash flow. It was a major punch.

The first time Jon picked up Aspen's insulin it cost $1,000. Insulin, needles, and test strips now top their regular shopping list. Every finger-prick test costs a few dollars, and Aspen needs to do them several times a day. There was also $600 for blood work and the $40,000 they owed for the ER visit and three days in the ICU.

The bright side: the ER and hospital were willing to wait until their insurance plan reimbursed them so they could pay the $40,000 in one payment without going out of pocket.

The brighter side: at the time this all went down, the Dales had been following the Four Rules for years. While they didn't have a surprise chronic illness fund, they were able to tap the reserves they'd accumulated in other areas to pay for Aspen's medical expenses. It was an adjustment, to be sure, but they were actually able to cover the bills (minus the $40,000) with the cash they had on hand.

The brightest: While Jon is a freelancer, his main client has him on an annual contract. The client was very supportive and paid Jon during the time he took off after Aspen's diagnosis. Their budget added extra assurance. The Dales were living off last month's income (more on that in Chapter 5), so they didn't have to worry about making ends meet even with their spontaneous new expenses. Aspen's diagnosis was a huge emotional hit for the family. Being able to stay together through the adjustment, without worrying about money, felt like an incredible gift.

Today their budget looks quite different than it did before Aspen's diagnosis. Aspen now has her own separate health insurance plan, which the Dales are paying for entirely out of pocket. It covers some things in full and other things at 70%. They're out of pocket about $7,000 a year for medical expenses, which they've fit into the budget.

Nothing could have prepared the Dales for Aspen's surprise diagnosis, and yet they somehow managed to be fully prepared—at least financially. With money stress out of the picture, Jon and Amy could put all their focus on Aspen and their three older kids. Sure, they were suddenly years away from hitting some Rule Two goals that they'd been just about to complete, but like Todd's garage door incident, the Dales' budget still fully reflected their values. They were taking care of their family.

Oh, Hi, Rule One

Remember when I said each of the Four Rules is actually Rule One for different scenarios? Surprise. Rule Three is literally just Rule One—all month long. You assign jobs on day one, and then you keep doing it as life unfolds. Even in extreme scenarios, like Aspen Dale's medical bills or Tracy Kellermeyer's layoff, Rule Three is just a matter of looking at the big picture of all your money and asking: *What do I want my money to do for me?* Then you start moving it around. You make a new plan.

All that moving is the reason we call Rule Three "Roll with the Punches." The original analogy comes from boxing. When your opponent throws a punch, you're less likely to get hit if you keep moving. You have to bob and weave, constantly adjusting your position based on what comes your way. Even if you do get hit, it will hurt a lot less if you move with the punch. The moment you stand still is when you're most likely to get knocked to the ground.

The connection goes well beyond boxing. I'm often reminded of sports when I think of budgeting, in large part because budgeting isn't actually a *thing*, it's an activity. Whether you're dodging blows or coming up with your game plan, you're always strategizing, adapting, and working to accomplish a big goal. You wouldn't think of just standing there. And like any challenging activity, you'll do your best only if you take care of yourself in the process. That means being kind to yourself when you need it, sticking to your values, and staying focused on the big picture.

If you don't allow yourself change, you're going to quit. What other choice is there when you're holding a bill that is more than you'd planned to spend? You can roll with the punches and reassign your dollars, or you can resolve that you're just not cut out for this. The latter might be tempting, but if you've read this far I'm going to guess you're not one for giving up that easily.

RULE THREE:
ROLL WITH THE PUNCHES

Repeat after me:

Changing my budget is not failing.

Changing my budget is not failing.

If you spend more than you'd planned, or a surprise expense hits that you weren't saving for, don't worry. Your budget is meant to reflect real life. When did anything in your life ever go *exactly* as planned? Just roll with the punches and keep going.

And remember: even if you don't hit all of your goals as you'd hoped, you'll probably see that your budget still reflects your values. So even if that $100 Little League registration was not on your radar, you'll pull it from other spending targets, like clothing or restaurants, because you value outdoor fun for your family. You're not failing—you're just budgeting in real life.

CHAPTER 5:

Rule Four—Age Your Money

We all want to feel less stress around money. It's a big reason we budget. But at what point can we draw a line in the sand that says, "From *this* day forward, my money stress is gone"? How can we know when it's truly okay to relax and stop worrying?

Here's a potential clue: a big pile of money sitting in your bank account. Okay, I'm being a little bit cheeky here. But won't we all be happy and stress-free when we have a nice fat bank account balance? Maybe. A heap of cash is a good start, and one that is bigger than what you had before is an even better start, but its powers depend on *how long that money has been sitting there*—and how long you can expect it to stay. If it's due to vanish the moment your next wave of bills hits, that money stress you thought was gone is actually right at your heels. One surprise bill or life event and it will catch up to you.

That's why having a bigger pile of money than you did before is important, but the actual amount isn't what makes the difference. It's also why you can't judge your own progress based on the size of your neighbor's money pile. What is important is that you have enough on hand so you won't be in trouble if your next paycheck doesn't arrive.

Rule Four: Age Your Money gets you to that point where you don't *need* your next paycheck. In fact, if YNAB helps put an end to financial stress, Rule Four is where you really start to feel that the relief will last. It helps you literally stockpile cash so you have enough of a reserve to cover your bills and spending for a long time. How long? That's totally up to you. But the older your money, the further away that money stress will be. Age your money long enough, and the stress won't even be in your line of sight.

What We Can Learn from College Dining Halls and Farmers

Remember the cereal station at your college dining hall? That colorful row of cereal dispenser towers was an oasis during long study nights, or when you couldn't stomach cafeteria mystery meat for dinner.

If I'm not describing your college years, think of the towers of by-the-pound nuts and candy that you can find at most grocery stores. Or even a grain silo at a farm.

Those dispensers all work in the same way: When new cereal (or gummy worms, or grain) is added, it's poured into the top and lands on the older cereal that was already there. When you want some, you take it from the bottom and the new cereal works its way down. The cycle keeps moving: newest at the top, oldest at the bottom.

If you eat cereal faster than the tower gets filled, it's going to run out. That's not a big deal if you have a whole row of other items to choose from, but what if we're talking about the only grain silo on a farm? If it's the community's one source of food, running out is a problem.

The best way to avoid running out of food is to take less than what is added each day. When that happens consistently, reserves build up out of the portions that are left over. Each day's leftovers slowly work their way down the tower as new cereal is added to the top.

You're living on the edge if you're eating cereal that was added that same day, or even the day before. It means you'll run out if you miss even one day of refilling your supplies.

But if you're eating ten-day-old cereal, it means you have a ten-day buffer between the time the cereal is added and the time you need it (don't worry, those chocolate-frosted sugar bombs are so loaded with preservatives, they'll last way longer than that). The bigger the gap between the time you put in the cereal and the time you take it, the more security, flexibility, and options you'll have if the unexpected were to happen. You want that cereal to age for as long as possible before you use it.

The Older, the Better

You can use Rule Four: Age Your Money to help you measure how "old" your money is. Money's "age" is based on the gap of time between when you **earned** the money (cereal in) and when you **spend** the money (cereal out). If the money you're spending on Tuesday was just deposited on Monday, your money is one day old. If it's Friday before you're spending that money you deposited on Monday, then your money is five days old.

Rule Four is more of a tool than a rule because we don't set an absolute standard for how old your money should be—just older. We tell people that thirty to sixty days is a good goal, but one day is better than no days; five days is better than one. Just keep working on increasing the time between receiving money and spending it.

If you're in debt the "age" of your money is actually in the negative. You spent your check before you even had it, either through credit cards or loans. But that doesn't change how Rule Four works—the strategy is the same. Spend less than you earn and use the difference to wipe out your debts. Once you have cleared that hurdle (and you will), instead of putting that extra money toward your debt payment, you have the luxury of letting it sit there and age. You're no longer paying for what you spent in the past. Now you're sending money to the future, so it's sitting there waiting to be spent later.

Also keep in mind that if you're spending money that you just earned yesterday, or even this week, you're living paycheck to paycheck. That's certainly better than being in debt, but just like eating the grain that was harvested today, it gives you little room for dealing with the unexpected. When you're spending money as soon as it comes in, you're mostly just putting out the fires in front of you. The goal is to slow down the cycle of money in and money out to give yourself breathing room between when you earn your money and when you need to use it.

Welcome Back, Sanity

It may sound odd to hear you shouldn't spend your paycheck when you get it. Isn't that how money works for most of us? Money comes in, we pay our bills, and we buy the things we need. This is reality for most people, and the idea of *not* needing that upcoming paycheck feels so impossible, we might as well wish to be millionaires.

That's what money stress is about, after all: the feeling that it's impossible to get ahead. It doesn't really matter how big or small your paycheck is. If money flies in and out of your account so quickly that you never have a chance to catch your breath, that stress exists whether you're earning $1,000 or $10,000 a month. You're stuck in the cycle of earning and paying, earning and paying. It feels like if you take one wrong step on the treadmill, you'll fall flat on your face.

The bulk of this stress is tied to living paycheck to paycheck, which is exactly what Rule Four helps you overcome. We spend our energy and our sanity trying to time bills to paychecks. We even trick ourselves into thinking that this kind of strategic juggling means we're being smart with our money because we're staying on top of our bills. But if you can build up your money to be at least thirty days old, that valueless game goes away because the month's money is already sitting there, waiting to be spent.

Put another way:

Without Rule Four, you've got a stack of bills waiting for money.

With Rule Four, you've got a stack of money waiting for bills.

Spending old money means all sorts of things for your health and sanity. For one thing, you'll actually get your sanity back because you won't be spending so much brain space and energy juggling bills. Imagine not having to wait for your next check to pay certain bills. Imagine putting them all on autopay knowing the money will actually be there. It's quite a feeling. You'll sleep better.

That relief comes when you don't need to use your money right away. This buys you time—time to make decisions, time to adjust, time to correct course. The longer you can wait to use your money, the more control you have. The less you can, the more circumstances control you.

That beautiful gift of time is especially valuable if you have a variable income. When you're living off old money, you don't have to take that crazy client just because this month is a bit short. You have a cash buffer. The more variable your income, the greater your age of money should be so you have a cushion to ride out the low-cash months.

And no matter your income scenario, aging your money helps you weather peaks and valleys. It gives you options on how to cover a cash shortfall or emergency. You'll be relieved knowing your expenses are covered for a span of time. You'll be more creative and less reactive no matter what kind of financial challenges might crop up.

Amazing Things Happen When You Take a Step Back

Have you ever looked back on a situation and realized it was much more stressful than you'd understood while it was happening? You got through it (somehow), but now that you've had some distance you can clearly see it was not ideal.

This tends to happen to us when we go on a much-needed vacation. Sometimes Julie, the kids, and I get so wrapped up in a crazy schedule of activities and obligations that we don't realize how stressed we are. We keep bouncing from appointment to appointment, collapse in our beds at night, and do it all again the next day.

We only notice the true effects of our wild routine after we've pulled ourselves out of it. When we manage to get away and find ourselves, for a blissful moment, doing *nothing* but watching the kids play, we realize: We're *tired*. Wow, are we tired. Just thinking about what we left back home is overwhelming: settling into our new house, sports practices, dance classes, homework, running a business, CrossFit goals (Julie and I are both a little obsessed).

Taking that step back is a huge help. It lets us see the full picture of our life and what we might want to change to make it more manageable. The last time this happened, we came home from vacation and canceled a dance class that our oldest daughter told us she'd grown tired of. Even at eight years old, a little distance helped her prioritize her life. We listened. We also got back on the wagon with simpler meal planning so we weren't always scrambling to figure out dinner each evening. Those little tweaks helped a lot.

Other times the distance led to huge changes: homeschooling for a year, changing my work routine, even the decision to move into a smaller house.

Rule Four gives us this same clarity when it comes to our money. It gives us *time* to look at the full picture of our cash flow so we can see what's working, and what's not. Again, it's that relief that comes with aging your money. It's nearly impossible to see clearly when you're living paycheck to paycheck. You're just surviving at that point. Rules One through Three absolutely help, but looking at a complete snapshot of your money from a distance brings a new layer of understanding to your money habits.

It's like jumping from activity to activity without a chance to realize how tired you are. You can't see how your habits are hurting you. Perhaps you'd be much happier and better rested if you just cut a few things out of your routine. Maybe you'd even perform better at work, be more patient with your kids, and have the energy to hit your workout goals if you cut out a few "obligations."

That's the problem: when you don't have the clarity to see how you're doing, you can't see the simple changes that would make things a whole lot better.

Alex Hatzenbuhler, a twenty-three-year-old software engineer in Minneapolis, had this exact realization a few months into his first full-time job.

When You Don't Know Where You Stand, You Don't Know What You're Capable Of

On the surface, Alex Hatzenbuhler's money story may seem boring (don't be fooled). He grew up in a financially stable home. He always had a job in college and enough money to go out with friends, buy games, or take off on snowboarding trips. He's been using credit cards since he was eighteen and always pays his full balances on time. No debt, no drama.

Alex graduated from college in June 2015 and immediately got a job coding at Target headquarters. Hello, adulthood! He now had a 401(k) and he was excited to start saving and investing for beyond retirement. The problem: he didn't know how much he could even afford to save or invest because he wasn't keeping track of his money.

Alex's four credit cards were also taking up most of his financial brain space during that time. While he's always used them responsibly, he got tripped up when it came to paying them. "I was scared to use autopay," he says. "What if money wasn't in the account I was paying from? What if I missed something and I didn't have enough money? There was always a level of uncertainty." Alex's solution was to set up Google Calendar events and reminders, and manually pay his credit card bills each month. It was a juggle.

Alex still managed to save 15% of his take-home pay in those first six months. Sounds pretty great, but he had a feeling he could do better. "I started to realize that money was important, but what was more important was managing that money," Alex recalls. He began reading more about budgeting and finance, and that's when he heard about YNAB in a reddit forum. He was quickly hooked on the Four Rules.

One year after getting his first paycheck, Alex's money picture drastically changed. The numbers tell all:

During his first six months of following the Four Rules, Alex saved 70% of his take-home pay. Up from 15% during the previous six months.

That isn't a typo. He jumped from saving 15% of his income to 70%. And he didn't do it by eating ramen noodles every day.

"Looking at those numbers, they almost seem fake," Alex admits. "But the only real change I made was thinking about my spending. Previously, I never thought about how much I was spending on anything. It's scary to think about now, because I don't know what I was spending my money on!"

Alex did review his last three credit card statements when he started YNAB to help ballpark his Rule One job assignments. That's when he discovered one of his big money pits—eating out.

Before YNAB, Alex spent about $450 a month on eating out. This included lunch/coffee at work and going out with friends. That's an estimate based on his previous three credit card statements.

After six months of YNAB, Alex knows, down to the penny, that his eating out average is $141.88 a month (exact number based on six months' worth of data).

"It blows my mind how much of a difference it makes eating out a few times a month rather than a few times a week,"

Alex says. After having this realization, he started bringing his lunch from home a lot more often.

Alex also adjusted many other habits that budgeting helped uncover, like buying tech gadgets he didn't truly need and spending way more on gaming than he'll ever care to admit. This quickly helped free up money for investing and building up a cash buffer. At the time of this writing, Alex is spending money that is more than two months old. He finished budgeting out January with a paycheck he received in mid-November. That buffer has a huge effect on Alex's state of mind.

"I never feel like I need a paycheck," he says. "Of course I'll always take it, but I'm not relying on the next paycheck to live, or even the next four paychecks. Even being a single paycheck ahead relieves so much stress and worry from day-to-day life."

Alex's financial buffer has also helped him relax about his credit cards. He still has all four cards because they each offer excellent rewards, but they're now all on autopay. He knows exactly how much he spends on what, and that the money is sitting in his account for when the bills land. Actually, the only time he thinks about his cards now is when he logs in to redeem his rewards.

The biggest boon comes in how much progress Alex has made on his investing goal. "Because I know exactly what my money is doing, I also know how much I can save or invest," he says. "I have a $100 deposit go into my investment account every week, and I know I can do that because I budget it ahead of time. The full picture is worth so much more than just pieces here and there."

Alex's experience is a great reminder of the power of taking a step back. Once his paycheck-to-paycheck stress was gone, he had the brain space to figure out the small changes he could make that would lead to huge results.

Not Just for the Superrich

I know aging your money can seem impossible if you're in debt or living paycheck to paycheck. Every dollar tends to already be claimed before it even hits your account. But really anyone can do this, no matter what your money situation.

If you want to be very intentional about aging your money, you can save for it separately. Know you spend $4,000 in a typical month? Chip away at saving $4,000. When you hit your goal, use that money at the start of a new month instead of your upcoming paycheck. There—now your money is thirty days old.

Whatever your approach, achieving your Rule Four goal boils down to consistently spending less than you earn. You've heard this before, I know. It's like being told that diet and exercise will help you lose weight. But both are true. Just like getting healthier, it helps to have a structure in place to get you there. In this case that structure is YNAB's rules.

Aging your money is really just a by-product of following Rules One through Three:

Rule One makes you more aware of what your money is doing and helps you to stop spending on things that aren't important to you. This gets you on the fast track to spending less than you earn.

Rule Two has a huge influence on the age of your money because it gets you saving for longer-term expenses. Since that money doesn't get spent right away, it sits there and grows old. Rule Two also helps you see that some future obligations are more important than current "wants." Setting money aside for next month's rent instead of eating out for lunch at work this week is deferring the use of your money. Those tiny decisions help keep your money in-hand, where it can sit and age.

And **Rule Three** keeps you adjusting and adapting, which will keep you budgeting over the long haul. Your money won't get a chance to age if you don't stay in the game for a while. Rule Three also keeps you accountable to the ultimate bottom line—which keeps you from going *backward*.

Go Short-Term Crazy

There's another solution if you want to age your money quickly: the sprint.

The sprint is a short period of time during which you go to extreme measures to accumulate extra cash. Once you've brought in enough to fund a month of expenses, you'll officially be out of the paycheck-to-paycheck cycle. Push yourself to the limits, and when you feel you can't do it anymore, remember this is only temporary. At the end of a sprint you collapse over the finish line. You don't want to run another step. You're not supposed to be able to maintain this for a long time. That's why it's a sprint. Some things you can try:

Get a second job. If child care doesn't make it practical to work out of the house, look for a work-from-home job. Then work while your kids sleep. WeWorkRemotely.com is a great site for finding reputable telecommuting jobs.

Pick up freelance work or do odd jobs. Scour websites that post gig work in your industry. Also get creative about leveraging your talents to bring in money. Are you strong? Offer to move stuff. Can you sew? Start tailoring other people's clothing. Are you handy? Can you paint walls? Fix computers? Install chandeliers? Plan great parties? We often take our talents for granted while others are willing to pay someone good money to do exactly what we do. Promote your services on social media. Create a website or post your services to gig boards. You could just end up with a little (or big) business on your hands.

Sell your stuff. Look around your house. Do you really need that jogging stroller now that your youngest was just bat mitzvahed? That treadmill you use as a drying tree for your delicates? Dig through closets and basements. Declutter your garage. I promise you'll find *so much stuff* you don't use. If you can't be bothered with garage sales or eBay listings, consider consigning your clothes. Sell your unwanted books on Amazon. Sell clothes and toys in lots on Craigslist or Facebook online yard sales. You won't get as much per item, but it's quicker and you can use the time you saved to earn more money through your side gig.

Get intense about not spending. Remember, this is a sprint. It's not meant to be permanent. You can do anything for a short period, right? Yes. Yes, you can. So get crazy about not spending for a month. I'm not talking about reducing expenses on things you don't care about. That's just budgeting. I mean stop spending on the things you like. Abolish nearly everything during your sprint. Don't just cut back on eating out—eliminate eating out. Don't go to the movies. Cut out any frills. Dig deep into your pantry for most of your food and only spend on essential perishables. Have fun for free: hike, bike ride, have a picnic with the treasures in your pantry.

Outsource your stuff. Think about things you own (that you didn't sell) that others would value. Do you have a van? Again, move stuff—or rent it to others and let them do the lifting. If you feel comfortable using services like Airbnb, temporarily rent out your home and stay with friends. You can leverage online networks to rent out just about anything: tools, bikes, cars, parking spots, clothing. You can even rent out your Wi-Fi connection. Google it.

If your sprint feels intolerable after a couple of weeks, you're probably moving at just the right pace. Keep going. You have a goal and you can do this. You'll go back to normal life soon. This will be worth it.

Find Hidden Windfalls—Then Budget, Budget, Budget

Celia and Cory Benton live in North Carolina with their three kids. They had been using YNAB for about a year and a half and had built a two-week buffer in their cash flow when their third child was on his way. That alone was a huge help. Before YNAB, they'd always done the timing-bills-to-paychecks dance, to much stress and aggravation.

Cory's full-time job as a lab tech manager covers most of their bills. He gets paid biweekly and one paycheck equals their entire mortgage payment. Cory's second paycheck of the month covers the rest of their expenses. It works in theory, except that before YNAB, much of their spending went on a credit card and they often didn't know whether Cory's upcoming paycheck would cover the balance plus other bills. That meant the occasional overdrafting for years before they started YNAB. They were eager for a break.

Enter their savior: the three-paycheck month. Cory gets paid every other Friday, which means a few months a year he actually gets three checks. A third paycheck landed shortly after they started using YNAB and Celia saw it as the lifesaver that it was. Their much-needed buffer! The moment the check landed, Celia budgeted it toward the *next* month's mortgage payment. Then the first check to arrive that following month covered the rest of their monthly expenses. And just like that, they were out of the paycheck-to-paycheck vortex. They were finally ahead. They're working on aging their money longer, but for now just those two weeks make a big difference.

But then a new challenge appeared: expenses for their son's upcoming birth. They had to pay for Celia's *and* the baby's insurance deductible, plus 20% of the birth's costs, in cash. Celia works part-time as a tutor and was able to take on extra hours to help save. They also cut their spending, but there was no way they'd have the full amount in time for the birth. That's when Celia started sleuthing.

"We needed a new windfall to help us reach our goal," Celia remembers. "I was looking through Cory's flex spending benefits when I remembered they have a wellness rewards program. If you hit certain goals they would drop money into your flex spending account."

Together, Celia and Cory reached every goal they could. Cory was rewarded $100 for using a step tracker and completing a walking challenge. They each got $150 for getting their annual physical. They were rewarded $300 each time they participated in wellness coaching by phone on topics like weight loss and exercise. And their biggest reward: $700 when Celia dialed in for a course on pregnancy. The program turned into a huge windfall for Cory and Celia. It was free money just sitting there, and it all went toward paying for the birth.

Remember that windfalls aren't just surprise inheritances or end-of-year bonuses. They're any cash jump: a tax return, a three-paycheck month, an employer benefit, the chance to take on extra hours at work. The point here isn't about the extra money (remember, it's not about the money!), it's about making a really intentional decision whenever something like this happens. Whether you're hustling to build a buffer or looking for ways to pay a big expense, it's those little upticks that will help you get ahead if you budget them to your top priorities.

RULE FOUR:
AGE YOUR MONEY

Living off "old" money can feel like a pipe dream if you're living paycheck to paycheck. Remember, this isn't a luxury reserved for the rich. Some things you can try:

• **Set a goal to save what you spend in a typical month.** When you hit your goal, budget out the new month with that money. Now your next paycheck can go to the *following* month. Your money is officially thirty days old.

• **Embrace the sprint.** Go on a no-spending spree for as long as you can. Also hustle to bring in extra cash in creative (and legal) ways. Anything you save or earn goes straight to your savings for the new month.

• **Budget windfalls to next month.** We all have them at some point. If your money isn't as old as you'd like, use a windfall to get ahead by budgeting it to a future month. The stress relief will feel so much better than the temporary happiness any new purchase can bring.

Remember, anyone can do this—it just takes a smart blend of goal setting, tenacity, and patience. It's totally worth it.

CHAPTER 6:

Budgeting as a Couple

If you've ever been in a relationship, you know how exciting those first milestones can be: first date (for Julie and me, it was sharing an entree at a nice restaurant), first kiss (in the thirty-year-old Honda), first time you get in a fight and realize she's not going to dump you for it (Monopoly, 2002). But first conversation about money? It usually doesn't make anyone's top-ten list. Let's be honest—it's often more of a dreaded elephant in the room than it is an exciting landmark.

Nobody is to blame or at fault for this—there's just so much opportunity for things to go wrong. You don't want to hear that the person you love is crippled by debt, or that he thinks credit cards are a super-convenient way to pay rent when his freelance checks are late. Or maybe that's *you*, and you know you need to do better, but you worry the truth about your financial situation will sour the good thing you have going. Plus, we've all heard the stats about how most relationships end because of disagreements over money. The topic just seems like a minefield of relationship woes.

On top of all that, people rarely talk to you about love and money. You get all sorts of advice about dating, marriage, how to raise kids if you're at that point in your relationship. But not about money, right? Most of us don't even know how to bring it up with our partner.

If you plan to spend the rest of your life with someone, you're going to have to talk about money at some point. And it won't be a single Band-Aid–ripping chat. You'll keep learning about each other's money quirks—your habits, your ideas about money, your impulses and dreams—over the course of your life together. You'll talk about money again and again and again, so it's worth getting comfortable with the topic.

So, how to take the pain out of the inevitable? Surprise— you (both) need a (shared) budget. If a budget sounds *worse* to you than talking about money on its own, hang with me. It really does help. On a very basic level, it's much easier to talk about your money when it's through the lens of a budget. Now it's not about your debt or my debt, my spending or your spending. It's about how it all works *within the budget.* The budget is like a neutral third party that keeps the conversation grounded in reality. Without a budget, our insecurities and misperceptions about money kill our chances of having honest conversations. Money is also constantly shifting, especially when two people are involved. A budget makes it all visible and less vulnerable to misunderstanding.

Above all, a budget gives you both a structure for designing your life together, and to talk about your hopes and goals within a concrete framework. You're no longer just dreaming together—you're working out a realistic action plan.

The mechanics of budgeting together are not all that different from budgeting alone: new money comes in, you assign jobs to those dollars, and you spend according to your plan. But the similarities end there. It's why I'm dedicating an entire chapter to budgeting as a couple.

To start, you can't come up with a plan for your money—or your life—unless you both agree to budget. That's where so many couples hit a wall. You may love the idea of a budget, while your partner sees it as a suffocation device. Just hearing the word *budget* may prompt fear and panic.

You say: Honey, I think we should start budgeting.

He hears: Honey, I think it's time I put you on a leash and start micromanaging your spending.

You say: Babe, I'd love to replace the old deck, too. Let's start saving up for it.

She hears: Babe, what makes you think we can afford to replace the deck? You know nothing about money management.

You say: Sweetie, I'm not sure we're spending our money where we should.

He hears: Sweetie, how about you stick to the allowance I've assigned to you this month?

The resistance may be fierce if your partner doesn't consider him- or herself the "financial type." He could be scared to learn the truth about his (and your) money, or argue that you don't need to budget since you're living comfortably and have cash in the bank. Others are so busy earning a substantial income, they don't want to be bothered with the minutiae of budgeting.

If you're struggling to convince your partner that budgeting is important, be sure you're very clear on what you mean by "budgeting." Nobody will be micromanaged or put on a leash. The point is to actually feel free and empowered. Budgeting together will mean you're working together to achieve your shared goals—not *your* goals for your partner. You're asking him to budget with you because you want him to have a voice in what happens with your money. Not the other way around.

Get to Know Your Money Partner

You learn so much about a person when you partner with them: their habits, their quirks, the things that drive them absolutely insane. And as your own idiosyncrasies unfold, you discover how they affect your partner. Maybe you didn't think anything of the fact that you always shower with music on, reserve Sunday nights for football, and like to iron your underwear. Seemed totally normal until you moved in together and learned that your 6 a.m. jam session annoys your partner, who doesn't need to wake up until seven. But the tides even out when you discover she also holds Sunday football sacred, and she doesn't really care what you do with your boxer briefs.

There's a learning curve to joining forces, no matter how compatible you think you may be. The same goes for when you start budgeting together. A budget makes you more aware of your money habits and expectations, especially in terms of how they affect your partner.

If you're living together and budgeting together, you'll quickly see there's a lot of overlap between the "learning to live with you" and "learning to budget with you" conversations. The spillover affects everything from the temperature at which you set your thermostat to your eating habits. Your idea of peace may involve freedom to order takeout most nights so you don't have to worry about cooking. Your partner may look forward to cooking each evening as a way to unwind. You can't get far in your arrangement without getting to know a few fundamental things about one another.

When it comes to money, there are three things you need to learn about your partner, and that they need to learn about you:

Your habits with money. What are your day-to-day money behaviors? Do you transfer money to savings the moment your paycheck lands, or do you save only if there's money left over at the end of the month? Are you obsessed with finding the best deals when you make a purchase, or do you take pride in buying designer items at full price? Do you aim to pay your credit card balance in full, or are you fine with paying the monthly minimum?

Your ideas about money. What's your big-picture view on money? If you start to hyperventilate when you have less than eight months' worth of expenses in the bank, and your partner pops open the champagne when he has enough on hand to cover rent and pizza, you should know this about one another sooner rather than later. It doesn't mean you're not compatible, but you will need to figure out a way for your different perspectives to co-exist.

What you're bringing to the arrangement. Whether you're each bringing a huge pile of debt into the relationship or a huge pile of cash, you need to talk about it. How will you deal with it? What will it mean for your budget? Will you want to help pay for your partner's student loans inside your shared budget? There are infinite ways to approach just as many scenarios. And it's important to recognize there are infinite opportunities for misunderstanding or even shame here. But being clear about your plan, your ideas, and your feelings is the only way forward, and you can decide together what reality will look like when your two worlds merge.

There's a lot to learn about each other as you ease into budgeting, so take it slow, and be honest with yourself and with your partner. You can learn the basics in a few conversations, but getting to know your partner's financial behaviors is a long-term adventure.

When Different Money Upbringings Come Together

Our individual approach to money sometimes stems from our upbringing. You may be shocked to learn about your partner's financial past, or thrilled that you share such similar backgrounds. Whatever the scenario, you can find a way to coexist once you know what you're each bringing to the table—from your debt balances to your habits.

Laura's parents were blue-collar Sicilian immigrants who

believed it was critical for their kids to understand "the value of a dollar." At her parents' nudging, Laura got her first after-school job working in a local curtain shop at fifteen years old. When Laura received her first paycheck, her mom immediately opened a joint checking account with her, as well as a joint credit card. Laura's starting bank balance was that first pay-check: $185.

Then the lessons began: *This is how you write a check for your credit card payment. This is how you subtract that amount from your checking account balance. This is where you look to find out exactly how much money you have left to spend (or save).*

Now, when Laura was fifteen, being aware of her checking account balance just meant knowing whether she could afford that new Pearl Jam CD. The stakes weren't very high—her crush on Eddie Vedder aside—but she carried her practical approach to spending into adulthood, where it had a huge influence on helping her make smart money choices when it really counted.

When Laura was growing up, her mom conveniently forgot to tell her that paying less than the full credit card balance was an option. Laura was taught that if you didn't have the money to pay your bill, you couldn't use the card. She thought this was just a fact of life (and, well, she was right). She eventually realized that accumulating consumer debt was technically an option, but by then the idea sounded absurd to her. She much preferred her only-spend-it-if-you-have-it approach. It was just easier.

In truth, Laura's upbringing was rare. Many people grow up in households where money is never discussed—especially

not with the kids. Laura's husband, Owen, remembers getting scolded when he was twelve because he asked his parents whether they were rich, poor, or middle class. He'd heard
these terms on the news and realized he had no idea where his
family fell on the spectrum. They lived in a comfortable house
and he never saw his parents flinch when it came to making
purchases. But he was clueless as to whether they were rolling
in cash or drowning in debt. Now, at age twenty-five, he still
doesn't know.

Owen got his first credit card in college by responding to a
direct mail offer. He loved that he could purchase whatever he
wanted and only had to pay the minimum monthly balance.
"This is financial freedom!" he thought. By the time he graduated he was several thousand dollars in debt. Thankfully the
swelling balance scared him enough to stop using the card.

When Owen decided to propose to Laura, he still owed
$7,000 on that credit card—and he was nervous about telling
her. He'd noticed how pragmatic Laura was with her spending.
He just had a feeling she wouldn't relate to his carefree days of
movie theater binges and wing crawls with his dorm buddies.
But he felt he couldn't ask her to marry him without sharing
the truth. It wouldn't be fair to her.

Breaking the news to Laura wasn't as scary as he'd thought.
She explained that most of her college friends flashed their
credit cards daily and she'd always wondered how they'd manage to pay the bill. The answer for most of them was: they
didn't. Rather than judging Owen, she saw his debt paydown
as a challenge to solve. *How could they get $7,000 reasonably*

quickly? She thought about the eight-year-old Honda he'd inherited from his grandparents. He used to drive it to campus, but now that they both lived in New York City, the car sat in his parents' driveway in New Hampshire. What if he sold the car to pay his credit card?

Owen was in. He'd put so much energy into worrying what Laura would think about his debt that he didn't have the mental clarity to consider how he could knock it out sooner. He rarely used the car. If they wanted to take weekend drives out of the city, they could easily rent one. He sold the Honda for $6,000 and immediately put it toward his debt. The $1,000 balance felt infinitely more manageable. And next up, he could focus on saving for a ring.

No matter how bad your money situation feels, push yourself to be honest with your partner. You never know—she may be just as worried about sharing her money situation with you. If your relationship is strong, your partner is likely to offer moral support, even if it's just to help you see your situation more clearly. And you can do the same for her. Remember, you're in this together.

Your First Budget Date

Remember your first date with your partner? Both of you on your best behavior, asking each other questions about your hopes and dreams. Actually listening, not looking at your phone even once while the other person was talking (of course you don't do that now, either).

Your first budget together should start in a similar way—with your first budget date. As you get into the swing of budgeting you'll have monthly number-crunching meetings (we still like to think of these as dates, though). But to start, your first date shouldn't involve numbers at all. Just focus on what we at YNAB like to call Rule Zero.

Rule Zero is the process of deciding what's most important to you. This is fundamental to budgeting. You can't get far into Rule One without having a good idea about what you value.

You can use your first budget date to explore Rule Zero in three ways: what's most important to you as an individual, what's important to your partner, and what you value together as a couple. These will evolve into your budget priorities, because when you're budgeting as a couple, your budget will have three sets of priorities: *yours*, *mine*, and *ours*.

The only way to reveal all those priorities is to talk. Think big. Be open. Share your hopes and concerns. These conversations do end up looking a lot like first date material, only now you don't have to worry as much about scaring the other person away. Your partner probably already knows if you're obsessed with collecting Star Wars action figures, and if she stayed with you anyway, she won't be surprised when you say it's a priority for you to allocate money to your collection. True love will prevail.

Again, you won't learn everything in one conversation, so use your first budget date to identify some broad priorities as individuals and as a couple. Do you want to rent a desk at a coworking space so you can finish your novel? Does your partner want to invest in coding classes so she can make a career change? Do you both want to save up for a house? Have a financial cushion for the baby that's on the way? Take an epic trip to Fiji? Forget the numbers and use this time to talk through what you want your life together to look like.

Don't worry if it takes you a while to get the hang of it. Talking about money isn't easy. Just give yourself plenty of time and lots of practice.

Navigating Yours, Mine, and Ours

Yours. Mine. Ours. You can't get far in a budgeting relationship without realizing that these three sets of priorities exist— and without talking openly about them. It doesn't matter how solid your relationship is. Assumptions will get in the way if you aren't clear with each other about what's important to you as an individual, and which goals you share as a couple. It's too easy to assume that *your* priorities are the same as *mine*. Or that *our* priorities are always more important than *mine*. These quiet assumptions are what make budgeting as a couple stressful when it absolutely doesn't have to be.

The key to keeping your priorities clear, and your budget stress-free, is communicating.

Sometimes it's hard to even decide whether a priority is yours alone, or one that you share. If it's something for you that will make you happier, healthier, or more successful, couldn't you argue that it would benefit both of you? Or even your whole family, if you have children? You can, and there's nothing wrong with making it a shared priority if you both agree that it is. But this approach might leave you with an overwhelming number of shared priorities crowding your budget.

I recommend boiling your priorities down to a small number of things—around one for each of you, and two that you share. You probably have more priorities than this but make an effort to zero in on your one selfish, personal priority. Then give each other more leeway to spend on that one thing. So maybe the baby cushion and Fiji trip turn into shared priorities, while the coworking space is yours. Meanwhile, the coding classes are your partner's. Perhaps you decide the house down payment is a shared priority, but you agree not to fund it for now because other things take precedence. It doesn't matter how you break things down as long as you're deciding together.

My friend Todd and his wife, Jessica, have been budgeting long enough that their budget dates are sort of rolling. It comes up a lot in their conversations (and in Jessica's teasing) that one of Todd's big personal priorities is running. He's an avid runner and needs to budget a fair amount of money for things like gear, massages, and traveling to participate in races. When Jessica started her own business, travel, conferences, and training became new personal priorities for her. It's important to Jessica to invest time and money in developing her skills and professional network so she can grow her business.

Todd could have argued that his running expenses are a shared priority, since running keeps him sane and makes him a better husband and father (and he does believe this). Jessica could have made an equal case that growing her business would make her a better wife and mother. So are they shared goals? In some ways, sure, but Todd and Jessica decided to set them as individual priorities. Jessica mostly thinks it's insane to spend so much on running shoes, but she trusts Todd. And Todd wouldn't begin to know the best way to invest in building Jessica's business, but he trusts her. So they leave those decisions to each other and focus their shared efforts on other goals. They both would love to renovate the upstairs bathroom and take their kids on another extended summer trip.

This works out for everyone: Todd gets freedom to spend on running, Jessica on her business, and they're both happy to prioritize savings for travel and renovations. And they'd compromise on other, less important goals as needed. There was no right way of breaking up the priorities—they just had to sit down and decide together.

The two big priorities Julie and I share are family vacations and weekly date nights. We love traveling with our kids, so we make a point of saving for at least one annual trip. We're also strict about keeping our weekly date, which includes paying a sitter to watch all six kids. (We tried getting twelve-year-old Porter to babysit once, but he just ended up bossing his siblings around. We're counting down to when eight-year-old Lydia is old enough to take over. She'll nail it.)

Sometimes our date is at a really nice restaurant. We love eating out, and since Julie is an excellent cook it doesn't feel worth the trouble unless we're eating food that Julie wouldn't make at home. Other times our date is a kid-free stroll through Costco. There's just something nice about being able to browse the aisles and eat our way through the samples without kids in the background arguing about organic bunny snacks. Is it just us?

One of Julie's personal priorities is nice furniture. If it were up to me I'd fill our house with Ikea furniture and forget about it. Julie is quite the opposite. She wants to love every piece of furniture we own. She would rather have an empty room than fill it with furniture she doesn't absolutely love. One can argue that furniture is a shared expense, just like Todd and Jessica's renovations, and in most ways it is. Julie and I decided to make it her personal priority so she can have total control over what furniture we buy. We also put way more toward that category than we would if it were treated like a shared expense.

For ages, my personal priority was the Tesla Model S we purchased last year. I'd saved up for it for years and I know I drove Julie crazy talking about it all that time. I think she was relieved when we bought it just so she wouldn't have to hear me obsess anymore. She couldn't care less about the cars we drive, so while it's a family vehicle, getting a Tesla was my priority. Now that we have it, my new personal priority is ski gear.

You're guaranteed to learn new things about each other once you start to embrace *yours*, *mine*, and *ours* priorities. You may also be surprised to discover how liberating it is to know that your personal goals—from the responsible to the quirky—have a firm place in your shared life plan.

One Shared Pile of Money

I stress the importance of *yours*, *mine*, and *ours* when it comes to the source of your priorities, but the exact opposite is true when it comes to the source—and location—of your money.

At YNAB we encourage couples to keep all their money in one joint bank account. The same goes for credit cards. Keep one, or if you prefer to each maintain your own credit history, limit cards to one each.

This isn't to say you're doing it wrong if separate accounts work well for you. As with everything else in your budget, you decide what works best. We mainly encourage using a joint account because of its simplicity. It's just easier to manage your money when there are fewer moving parts. Four credit cards are harder to manage than one, even if you're perfectly within your budget. And all that management detracts from important decision making and often leads to decision fatigue. Instead of talking about goals and aspirations, you get stuck talking about the mechanics of where money came from, where it needs to move, and so on.

Technicalities aside, joint accounts also keep you from worrying about who earned what money. You've committed to being partners for life. It doesn't matter who earned what. It's one shared pool of money that is funding your shared life together. Embrace that and support one another on the journey.

TACKLING STRESS WITH YOURS, MINE, AND OURS

You know Celia and Cory Benton from Chapter 5. Shortly after their buffering strategy got them out of the paycheck-to-paycheck cycle, Celia and Cory sat down to revisit their priorities. They were thriving on their budget but Cory always resisted talking about the numbers, and at the same time, Celia needed to talk numbers to feel confident. Their talk turned into an honest vent about what each wanted their life to look like. While their priorities were quite different from one another's, they all shared the same theme: Celia and Cory both wanted their budget to reduce their stress.

Their shared priority was debt paydown. They agreed they'd both be less stressed if they knew they were making solid progress on their debt. Done.

Cory's biggest priority was to not have to deal with the budget. Seriously. Cory suffers from anxiety and depression, and money talk adds to his stress. Celia runs the budget and she knew Cory didn't like discussing it (that's why she suggested a priority check), but she didn't realize just how much budget talk bothered him. Knowing that actually *not having to talk about it* was a priority in itself was a huge help for Celia. With their shared debt paydown priority intact, she knew that any other Rule One decisions she made were fair game.

"As a trade-off for not having to deal with the budget, Cory is fine with whatever money decisions I make," Celia said. "He'll understand if there isn't money where he wants it to be. If we don't have restaurant funds one month, he knows it's because higher priorities needed the cash. It works for us. He's calmer, and I no longer stress about what he might think about a certain money decision. He's happier when I don't ask him."

For Celia, her stress-reducing priority is to have someone

help clean the house. Cory agreed, and house cleaning is now a part of their budget's Bills section. "We agreed that when I budget, the house-cleaning category comes before any nonessentials. Unfortunately we haven't fully funded our first cleaning session yet, but just knowing it's a budget priority is a stress reliever for me. It feels so great every time I move money to that goal."

Keep Up Your Monthly Budget Dates

Okay, so you do eventually need to sit down and look at the numbers together. But I promise it doesn't have to be a painful session of who-spent-what and what-were-you-thinking. That is the last thing it should be.

You need these sessions to be a safe space where you can talk openly, listen to your partner, and compromise. Yes, you're crunching numbers, but remember that this is really about staying on track to hit the goals you'd set together. Keep the vibe warm by treating your monthly powwow like a date (*not* a meeting). Curl up on the sofa with the iPad. Bring cocoa. Go to a cafe and talk about how you're doing over dessert.

I know this sounds like it's easier said than done. And it's true: your money conversations won't be warm and honest just because I tell you they should be. The only way to capture that vibe during your date is by making your budget a part of your daily life together. If you're both motivated to hit your goals, you'll see that this happens pretty naturally.

Maybe you'll look at your budget only once a month, but sharing one will color your conversations and behavior all the time. Sometimes you'll acknowledge it outright, when you say things to your partner like, "Ooh, I can really go for takeout sushi tonight. But I'd rather put that money toward our trip next month." Or when you strategize your grocery list together so you can stay within your monthly goal. Other times it will be unspoken, like when you both pause googly-eyed in front of the Costco TV displays (always as soon as you walk in). You stop for a second, then keep walking because you both know your not-so-smart TV is just fine, and you'd much prefer to put that kind of money toward the refrigerator you're saving up for (just a few aisles down).

You're executing your strategy in every one of those daily interactions. And like any team, you'll become stronger the more you connect on your plan. Think about it: a pilot and air traffic controller may agree on certain decisions while on the tarmac, but they also need to stay in communication while the flight is en route so they can adjust the plan as needed. Likewise, you can't expect your budget to work if you talk about it only once a month. You need to communicate as your spending decisions unfold.

If you're in touch about your budget daily, your monthly talks will be relatively easy, maybe even feel like an extra. Thirty minutes should be plenty of time to recap the prior month and set a plan for the one ahead. You'll get better at this the more you do it. After a few months your budget talks may only take ten or fifteen minutes (but hopefully the *date* portion will last much longer).

Let the Four Rules guide your sessions. If you're just starting out, set your priorities (after your Rule Zero date) and then roll on **Rule One**. Assign dollars to jobs together so you're both aware of your monthly targets. You may be guessing at certain spending categories, like fuel or groceries, in your first couple of months. That's fine! You'll get a realistic view of your spending the longer you budget together. Soon enough your monthly dates will turn into strategy sessions for hitting your goals.

You'll naturally veer into **Rule Two** as you set priorities and assign dollars to jobs. Set long-term savings goals together and be honest with one another. If your partner is feeling fierce about paying off the car loan but you're more concerned about saving for a much-needed trip, talk it through. Remember the three sets of priorities (yours, mine, ours) and explore how unspoken assumptions might be causing friction.

Also be open to the idea that priorities change. Maybe your partner was excited to save for that trip when you first started budgeting, but seeing your real-life spending over two months changed her mind. Now she's more concerned with killing your debt to free up future cash. You'd never know this unless she outright told you. And she might not tell you if she didn't feel your monthly session was a safe, open space in which to share her concerns.

Rule Three will make a showing at your monthly budget dates, but its true place is in the day-to-day. It's the "Gah, we blew through our grocery budget and it's only the seventeenth!" conversation. The "I know we said we wouldn't spend on clothes this month but I'm having dinner with the CEO and my best pants don't fit" conversation. The "How did we forget to budget for your mom's birthday?" conversation. You'll roll with the punches as you revise goals at your monthly pow-wow, but Rule Three was never meant to speak up only once a month. If one of you notices you've strayed off course, or that life isn't agreeing with your budget, take a moment to decide together how you're going to pivot—no matter what day of the month it is.

Rule Four is a great tool for measuring how well you're doing overall. You can get a quick pulse check on your money's age just by observing how you talk about upcoming paychecks. You'll know your money is not old at all—perhaps its age is even in the negative—if you keep looking to that next check to even out your budget. Those conversations might look something like this:

"When your/my next check lands, we'll be able to . . .

". . . budget out the rest of the month.

". . . send money to the category we've overspent.

". . . pay the bill that's due next week."

If this is you, don't worry. The fact that you're budgeting together will get you out of the paycheck-to-paycheck cycle and help build a cushion of older money. Just keep chipping away at your goals.

As your money ages, you'll see that your view on upcoming paychecks totally changes. You're no longer counting down the days until that check lands and rescues you. Now you have choices. You can do whatever you want with it! Fund future months if that's what gives you a thrill. Pour it into big savings categories to hit those goals sooner. You have time, breathing room, and freedom—use it for more conversations with your partner. Your budget meeting becomes less about strategizing how to make ends meet, and more about seeing your dream life unfold.

The Power of Personal Fun Money

There's a misconception that budgeting is all about restricting yourself. Being on a budget means no more eating out. No more stress-relieving strolls through DSW—not even the sale section. You know by now that this isn't true, that it's actually important to budget for the things that bring you joy.

The same goes when you're budgeting with a partner, only we encourage couples to up the ante by having a no-questions-asked "personal fun money" stash for each of you. We still want you to have those joy-inducing categories—eating out, shopping, whatever. But "personal fun money" is a little different. In this case, neither of you has to answer to the other about what you did with your loot. If you decide to fold yours into origami cranes and fly them off a cliff, that's your choice. You're still budgeting together when you do this because you're agreeing on how much "fun money" you'll each get. The rest is up to you. It's similar to budgeting for those impulse buys I mentioned earlier. Even though the spending itself is on a whim, it's still planned.

Budgeting fun money is a lot like working to be superefficient with your time but then allowing yourself room to gaze out the window. There is value in the gazing, too.

It doesn't matter how little you budget for this. When Julie and I started out we each literally had $5 in our fun money category, but it still made a huge difference. There was just something about having the freedom to do *whatever we wanted* with it that made the hard budgeting days more tolerable. We still do this today (I'm happy to report that we get more than $5 now) and we'll never give it up.

Do this for yourselves. Yes, set your goals and hustle to keep them, but make room for the origami cranes. The impulse drive-through milk shake when your restaurant budget is drained. The gazing out the window when you have so much to get done.

BUDGETING AS A COUPLE

I promise that budgeting as a couple isn't as scary as it seems. Keep these essentials in mind and you'll keep the (budget) love alive:

• When you start budgeting, get to know each other's habits with money, ideas about money, and what you're each bringing to the arrangement.

• Set regular budget dates and keep them fun (you can even budget for them!). The money talk likely won't last long, so also use the time to discuss your goals for the life you want to build together.

• Set *yours*, *mine*, and *ours* priorities, plus some no-questions-asked fun money for each of you.

• Combine your bank accounts and credit cards if you can—it means less time juggling bills and accounts so you can focus on making great decisions together.

CHAPTER 7:

Slaying Debt, Whatever Your Situation

I've spent this book being pretty even-keeled. You know by now that I won't tell you what to do with your money. Your priorities are your own, and the Four Rules are designed to help you get more clarity on what you want and how to get it. I'll never judge your spending decisions as long as you genuinely have the money to spend. Diamond dog collar, NASA-quality drone, whatever. If it makes you happy and you've set aside the money for it, buy away.

But I admit I lose my cool when it comes to debt. Fine—I get crazy. It's the one time I *will* tell you what to do, and I'd shout it through a megaphone if I knew it would make a difference. You know what I'm going to say. I already said it earlier:

Get rid of it.

If you're reading this book, I probably don't need to convince you to pay down your debt. Tackling debt is a big reason many people experience that "I need a budget" moment. But I want to be clear with you about *why* I think debt is such a problem. Most money gurus would tell you it's all the interest you'll pay. Paying interest isn't great, but it's only a small part of the problem.

My issue with debt is that it *restricts your cash flow*. It keeps money away from your priorities as you pay hundreds (sometimes thousands!) of dollars a month for something that's already happened. That's the exact opposite of what YNAB wants you to do. YNAB wants you to make choices for what's happening now, and in the future. You have jobs you want your dollars to be working on. But when debt is in the picture, it claims those dollars before they even hit your bank account. Your choices are restricted. Consumer debt is the biggest offender because most of it is for stuff you didn't even care about. And your present-day priorities are hurting because of it.

Debt Is Not an Option

Debt is not an option. Let this be your new mantra. Debt is not an option. Record and play it in a continuous loop if you have to, because once you pay off your debt you cannot slide back into it. If your goals feel too big, or bills too overwhelming, stand firm in believing that debt is not an option—then push yourself to figure out a solution. This is the exact thinking that spurred me to start YNAB back when Julie and I were trying to pay our bills and save for a baby. I wouldn't consider borrowing money, so I got the idea to try selling YNAB as a spreadsheet. It changed everything. If you fiercely believe that debt is not an option, you will find another way to hit your goals.

This is the point where the arguments come flying: *But what about a mortgage, or student loans? Some necessities are too expensive to pay for in cash. And there is such a thing as good debt!*

I hear this a lot. I do agree that not all debt is created equal. The worst *by far* is consumer debt, for the reasons I mentioned. The rest, however, still isn't great, again for the reasons I mentioned. My rule of thumb for deciding whether a debt is "good" or "bad" is whether the thing for which you're borrowing will go down in value. Borrowing for a new car is always a bad idea, since its value decreases the second you drive it off the lot. The margins on your losses are smaller with a used car but it's still bad debt if you need a loan to buy it.

Houses generally don't drop in value unless you're buying in a bubble (or selling in a crash). I still pay off my mortgages at a fever pace, but if there were ever an argument for "good" debt, mortgages make a fair case under the right circumstances. That means borrowing for a house that is well within your means, with a loan structure that fits comfortably within your budget. Now, I mentioned on page 46 that I disagree with financial advice that tells you to spend no more than X% on housing. That kind of guidance is blind to too many factors that may influence your decision (commuting costs, etc.). So when I say a potential mortgage should fit "comfortably within your budget," you're the only one who can decide what is "reasonable" based on your bigger life picture. If you can get clarity on what your true priorities are, you'll get clarity on what a reasonable mortgage is for you.

You also already know how I feel about student loans (ahem, page 72). It's absolutely possible to get a great education without borrowing for tuition. I did it, and I plan to teach my six kids how to do it. But is it "good" debt? Well, a college degree doesn't go down in value, though you need to be very careful here. Whether the numbers fall in line with your life's passions or not, many industries and areas of study do not give much of a "return" on that debt you've assumed.

But I get it: many of you are past college age and you're stuck with your loans. That's fine, and beating yourself up about past decisions is pointless—just focus on killing the debt. If you have kids, or plan to have them, give them the gift of taking debt out of the college-planning equation. The government and private lenders have spent millions trying to make us believe that student loans are inevitable. They succeeded. It's horrible. FAFSA posters hang in every high school as if they're required reading. Student debt has become as common as hangnails.

Debt is not an option. I stand by this mantra but I also recognize that you may be a long way from living debt-free. Eighty percent of Americans have debt of some kind. Younger generations feel it the hardest: 89% of Gen Xers and 86% of Millennials have debt.[*] It's okay—just get fierce about paying it off, then wield Rule Two like a maniac to stay out of it.

---

[*] Pew Charitable Trusts, "The Complex Story of American Debt," July 2015, http://www.pewtrusts.org/~/media/assets/2015/07/reach-of-debt-report_artfinal.pdf.

WHY THE BIG RUSH TO PAY OFF MY MORTGAGE?

Questions usually fly when I tell people that Julie and I race to pay off our mortgages. They wonder if it's part of some amazing money trick they should get in on. Technically, yes, you save a ton on interest if you pay off your mortgage faster than your loan term. You can easily find online calculators that show you how much you'll save on interest depending on how quickly you pay. But that's not why we do it.

Our big motivator has nothing to do with financial strategy. Julie and I just love the idea of living in a paid-for house. Nothing beats it. You can do math with it all day long, but at the end of the day, it's just awesome not to have a mortgage payment.

We had set the goal when I was twenty-five to pay off our first home before my thirtieth birthday. We pulled it off with eight months to spare. We're back to having a mortgage now but we hope to pay it off in three years. Again, no fancy financial strategy here—just a decision that it's one of the highest-priority jobs for our dollars. We just love living in a paid-for house, so we prioritize our spending to make it happen fast. Simple as that.

Not So Fast—True Expenses First

So you're with me. You're going to pay off your debt. You won't regret it—but it's important that you go about it the right way. As much as I despise debt, I'm actually not telling you to jump right into crushing it. It would be great if you could, but start by figuring out what you can truly afford to pay *after* budgeting for your obligations and other top priorities. Remember: many of your Rule Two true expenses are top priorities, even if they don't happen every month. Don't ignore them. If you do, you're likely to slide right back into debt the moment a "surprise" bill hits. You will get a flat tire. Your family will expect holiday gifts. You kind of can't ignore your boyfriend's birthday (really, you can't). Once you've built up a cushion for these inevitables, you can make your debt payments without worrying about getting blindsided later.

Rule Two is your debt antidote. Use it to figure out what you can afford in debt payments. Then keep using it to keep yourself *out of debt forever.* Just think about how Rule Two and debt work:

With **Rule Two**, you're assigning money now for spending that will happen later.

With **debt**, you're spending money now that you won't have until later.

Rule Two gets you ahead. Debt pulls you behind.

Everything goes back to freeing up cash flow for now, and for the future. Remember this especially if you're paying off multiple debt balances. Many "get out of debt" advocates and debt snowball systems recommend that when you pay off one debt, you immediately roll 100% of what you were paying on that first debt into another one. Maybe that will work for you— but don't be so quick to forfeit that freed-up cash.

First look at your budget: Could you use that money to fund any of your true expenses more robustly? Have any new priorities come up that didn't exist when you first started paying off your debt? If you decide your remaining debt *is* your most pressing priority, then sure, roll that cash flow into another balance. But it isn't automatic. You're in control.

For this reason, we recommend paying off your lowest-balance debt first if you have multiple debts. We want you to shrink the number of payments you're on the hook for each month so you have more freedom to decide how to use your money. It all comes back to simplicity. The fewer things you're juggling—whether they're bank accounts or debt payments—the more clarity you have to focus on what's most important to you.

Debt Hack: Using Rule Four to Nix the Stress

Mitchel Burton wrapped up his senior year of college like most Millennials: excited to take on the world, but more than a little concerned about the student debt that came with his diploma.

He assumed his loans were big, but he didn't actually know how much he was on the hook for until he looked up his balance for the first time that spring of 2011: $104,000.

He was floored. "I couldn't believe it. I felt sick to my stomach. I called my parents, 'Do you realize we signed up for more than $100K in loans?'"

But Mitchel loves a challenge, so he decided to slay his student debt as quickly as possible. He started working full-time months before graduation and dumped all the cash he could into his loan payments.

"I was earning $45K at that first job, which netted me about $2K a month. I pushed myself to put $1K toward my loans but I still had to pay rent on my studio apartment in downtown Chicago and cover my other expenses. I was putting myself in a tight spot and I was freaking out about money all the time."

Most of us know this feeling. Even if you've never faced Mitchel's exact scenario, that stressful dance of timing bills to paychecks is too familiar. It's the fallout from living with margins that are just too tight. The tiniest slip-up can throw you into credit card debt—and in Mitchel's case, that would have added more stress to the penny-pinching circus he'd already created for himself.

Mitchel knew he couldn't survive on the financial edge for long, so he went looking for a solution. That's when he found YNAB.

"Rule Four was the game changer for me," he said. "A month into using YNAB I was living off of my previous month's income. Knowing I had cash on hand to cover all of the month's bills was a huge stress reliever."

So how did he jump from counting quarters for a jar of Jiffy to having a full thirty-day buffer just a few weeks later? Strategy—and survival.

"I was dealing with layers on top of layers of stress. There was the stress of being in debt. Then there was the stress of living paycheck to paycheck and figuring out what I could afford in the day-to-day. That real-time dollar juggling was crushing me. I knew I was going to burn out if it didn't stop."

Mitchel mastered Rule Four by taking a hiatus from his aggressive debt payments and putting that money toward his thirty-day buffer. His spending was still tight, but knowing it was for the purpose of building his buffer made the penny-pinching more tolerable. His end goal was not far (much closer than paying off that $104,000), and he says building that cash reserve made all the difference.

Once he stopped worrying about whether he could afford to buy his week's supply of peanut butter and jelly and Jack's frozen pizza, he had the mental capacity to focus on his goals. That's when his aha moment hit: he needed to earn more money.

"I was happy with my paydown progress but I realized I was only going to get so far on my current salary. I was spending so much time and energy trying to eke every dollar I could out of my budget, but I was much better off putting that energy toward trying to earn more money."

With this new insight, Mitchel broke out of the comfort zone that was his first postcollege job and began interviewing. When he got a new position, his salary jumped from $45K to $65K. Over the next two years he negotiated two raises at that job, finally landing at a $90K salary. He was also taking on freelance work to earn extra money, which brought in around $10K/year. During this whole time he kept living like he was earning $45K, and every extra buck went to his loans.

It's worth noting here that the specific numbers aren't important. Mitchel is fortunate to make a good salary, but you could make the same progress jumping from a $25K to $30K salary, or wherever your income falls on the spectrum. The point is to keep your spending habits the same even when your income increases. Don't let lifestyle creep steal your raise by convincing you it's okay to let loose a little. Stay focused on hitting your big goals.

What's also interesting is that Mitchel first slowed down in order to speed up. He was throwing everything at his debt and that didn't work. So he took a step back, figured out what would work best for him, and *then* pushed forward.

Mitchel's original goal was to pay off his student loans before he turned thirty. He did it by age twenty-seven. While Rule Four was the linchpin, he credits his success to a few other key factors:

Rule Two: "Saving for true expenses is a big reason I was able to stay on track. I'd tried other budgeting solutions but nothing like Rule Two existed in those systems. I'd get stressed and depressed every time an infrequent expense hit. The holidays were the worst. Of course, I could have decided not to give gifts and be a jerk to everyone, but that didn't feel like a real option. So I put less into my loans in December and I hated it. I also love to travel and Rule Two helped me budget for that even while I was paying off my loans."

Raising your income game: "I think a lot of people forget the income side of the equation. Sure, being frugal works, but hustling to squeeze dollars that aren't there takes time and energy that you could put toward making more money. That's one of the biggest lessons I've learned: cutting down expenses will help to a point. If you want to move quickly with anything financially, it helps to get your income up. You have to be strategic about it. Just as you put plans in place for your budgeting goals, put plans in place for your income goals."

Remembering the big picture: "Budgeting turned me into

a cheap bastard and I'm totally okay with that. I've just come to value long-term goals way more than any possible short-term thing. I'm even a little neurotic about it at this point. Now that I'm out of debt I'm saving to buy a house. If I'm tempted to buy something unnecessary at the grocery store I stop myself. I'd just much rather have that money go toward the house than to a bag of chips. Maybe I'll treat myself once I hit my goal, but for now, I prefer to see my savings grow."

These days Mitchel works at a mortgage company, and the irony runs deep. That house he's saving for? He plans to buy it *in cash*. He hates the idea of going back into debt, even for something like a mortgage (don't tell his boss!). So he's keeping up with his $45K lifestyle, despite the fact that he now earns over $120K. The rest is stashed for his dream home. I have no doubt he'll get it even sooner than he's planned.

Big Effort = Big Progress

I know it's not practical for most of us to pull a Mitchel: throw more than half your income into debt payments and live on Wonder Bread. It's not always simple to double your income, either. No matter how it sounds, though, don't dismiss either one too quickly. Common sense tells us that we can't accomplish any goal (financial or otherwise) without putting in the effort. If you're carrying big debt balances and you're serious about getting rid of them, you'll need to make life changes. At the very least, you have to break the lifestyle habits that got you into any consumer debt you may have.

Progress tends to catch fire—this is especially true when it comes to paying off debt. The more you accomplish, the more you want to accomplish. There's just something about seeing your debt-free life come into focus as your balances shrink. You can quickly go from digging yourself out of a money hole to piling up mountains of cash. It's what happened to Mitchel, and it's the same scenario that Tracy and Dan Kellermeyer found themselves in after their big debt dig-out.

You read in Chapter 4 about how Tracy and Dan's budget survived a job loss. Before they saved up the emergency fund they didn't even need for that particular emergency, Tracy and Dan were obsessive about saving to pay for their upcoming wedding in cash. Their big goal: save $25,000 in the eighteen months leading up to their wedding and stay debt-free. Speaking of commitments, this was a big one.

"It took a *lot* of sacrifice," Tracy recalls. "We both moved home so our spending on rent, utilities, and groceries was low or nonexistent. And so was our privacy! But it meant we could live on about a third of our income. The rest was going to debt and savings. Our day-to-day lives during this time, to be honest, were pretty boring."

Tracy and Dan had to get creative when it came to hanging out with friends and going on dates. "Basically, we did as much as we could at home. Movie and wine nights, dinner dates in. If we wanted to go out, we'd opt for Starbucks instead of a restaurant. We didn't buy clothes or go out partying like the rest of our friends. When it got frustrating we reminded ourselves it was only temporary."

And then their progress caught fire. A couple of months into saving for the wedding, they decided to kick things up a notch. Tracy vowed to pay off her $21,000 car loan before the wedding, too. Meanwhile, Dan committed to paying off his $30,000 credit card debt before the big day. By the time their wedding arrived they were debt-free with enough cash on hand to pay for their wedding and honeymoon. Eighteen months of effort let them start their marriage with a clean financial slate.

I know it's easy to dismiss stories like Mitchel's or Tracy and Dan's if your life looks nothing like theirs. We can't all move in with Mom and Dad. Some of us need to live on more than peanut butter and jelly. But their efforts deserve our attention. Before each of them started on their debt paydown journey, reaching the end seemed impossible. But they set their goals and put in the work every day, consistently, for a long time. The equation is simple—the effort is hard. Don't let that stop you. Nobody has ever accomplished anything great without consistent hard work.

When Debt and Life's Punches Collide

Holly MacKenzie knew she couldn't get out of her financial jam without hard work and a little creativity. When she broke off her wedding engagement in the spring of 2014, she had a few logistics to work out. The big one: paying her living expenses on her own. She works full-time as a civil engineer in Maine but her salary alone didn't cover her bills. She'd have to find a way to bring in more income. Her quick solution was to rent out a room in her house. Money was still tight, but it worked.

Fast-forward to the following spring. Holly's roommate was preparing to move out and she was back to the same financial riddle. She didn't want a new roommate this time. Holly also knew that a bigger problem was at the root of her conundrum— her spending.

Holly had a thing for Target. In particular, she had a way of walking through those bright red doors for eggs and walking out with new workout clothes (or dishes, or a Keurig machine). Her strategy was to put big purchases on a credit card, because she was scared to see hundreds of dollars leave her bank account at once. Between paychecks, her checking account would be down to a few dollars and often overdraft. The line of credit attached to her account saved her every time. She'd pay it back with the next paycheck and start the cycle over again. Meanwhile, her credit card balances swelled.

Holly knew her spending habits were keeping her from being able to afford her mortgage. News of her roommate's upcoming move spurred her do something, but she had no idea what. She'd heard her coworker talk about her budget but Holly wasn't convinced. "I couldn't grasp the concept of something like a food budget," she recalls. "Really? A limit on what you eat?!" But she was terrified of not being able to afford her mortgage, so she decided to try it.

Setting up her budget stirred something in Holly's brain. As an engineer, she loves to crunch numbers and she loves to solve problems. Her budget was the perfect marriage of both those things. She was hooked.

Another little detail about Holly: her work ethic is fierce.

When she's not at her engineering job, she works a second gig as a Beachbody Coach (hence her love for workout gear). Once her budget was under way she got crazy about paying down her $10,000 credit card balance. She tackled the problem by working harder at her side hustle and going nuts on Rules One and Two.

"I try to squirrel money away in categories and expect the worst," she says. "When I started budgeting, I put money in the car repairs fund so when my old Jeep broke down, I had money waiting. I always put extra in my mortgage category so when repairs are needed, it is there. If something came up when I was working on debt payoff, I simply put the brakes on those payments and cash-flowed the expense."

Holly's credit card debt was gone within five months. By that point she had enough money on hand to comfortably cover her mortgage, Christmas gifts, *and* a trip to Punta Cana, Dominican Republic, in cash. She also cash-flowed the $1,000 registration fee on a 2016 Toyota 4Runner after trading in her ailing Jeep.

Next up—her $8,000 student loans. Holly made the final payment in May 2016 (less than a year after starting YNAB), leaving just her new car loan as her remaining debt. Oh, but she's on track to pay off the car in half the loan's time frame.

Holly's financial accomplishments have given her a huge boost of confidence, which only helps her achieve more. "I honestly feel that if I can change my spending habits and get out of credit card and student loan debt, I can do anything," she says. "My work as a Beachbody Coach is commission based.

I'm driven to want more from my business to put more in my budget. I've become extremely financially motivated (of course I want people healthy, too!). My budget has made me a better entrepreneur, leader, and businesswoman."

Holly started budgeting with under $1,000 to her name and $18,000 in debt. She now has well over five figures in her bank account. She pays for vacations in cash, spoils her team of fellow Beachbody Coaches, treats her family, and most important, doesn't stress about money.

SLAYING DEBT, WHATEVER YOUR SITUATION

*D*ebt is not an option.

Embracing this motto will change your life. Even if you're not buried in debt now, it will help you avoid it in the future. As you get ready for debt-free bliss, remember:

• Fund your **true expenses first**. There's no use in dumping all your cash into debt payments if it will leave you broke when new bills come in. True expenses are especially tricky when you leave yourself little cash. One surprise bill or expense, and you'll slide back into debt.

• You can't make big progress without **big effort**. Maybe you can't live on Wonder Bread (fair enough), but you can find creative ways to spend less—or earn more! Put in the work consistently over a long period of time. You'll get there, and it will feel *so* worth it.

CHAPTER 8:

Teaching Your Kids to Budget

I know this chapter won't apply to everyone, but the topic of kids and money is so important that I had to write it for the readers who do have children.

Talking about money with kids is not easy. Whether you're wealthy or you're struggling, it is hard to know what to say to give your kids a healthy outlook. You don't want to worry them if finances are tight. You don't want to make them think they'll never need to work for money if they do have a trust fund waiting for them. It's just as difficult if your means fall somewhere in between.

New York Times columnist Ron Lieber wrote an excellent book about raising kids who are smart with money called *The Opposite of Spoiled.* Among his advice is a deep dive into how to talk with kids about money. I won't try to duplicate Ron's efforts here. In fact, after reading Ron's book and interviewing him for the YNAB podcast, I use his advice with my own six kids (well, five of the six, since Faye is only a year old). What I *will* do here is show you the practical ways in which Julie and I help our kids develop a smart relationship with money. I hope this glimpse into our family life will help you find a healthy money rhythm with your own kids. Ron's advice is part of our inspiration, and not surprisingly, so are the Four Rules.

What, you thought we wouldn't teach our kids the Four Rules? (Of course you did.)

But before we get to the Four Rules, each kid needs cash. I'm a big advocate of giving kids an allowance so they can start learning how to manage money early. Keep the amounts small and you won't need to worry about spoiling them with handouts. At least, my experience proves that the reverse will happen. Giving your kids a modest allowance will help them immediately see that money is a finite resource. If they want to buy something, especially something big, they'll need to make smart choices with their money.

Julie and I start each kid on YNAB when they turn eight years old. Until then, the little ones get a cash allowance with which they can do whatever they want. Our five-year-old daughter, Rose, kept her dollars under her pillow for about three months. We tried talking her into using a better system but she insisted on the pillow. Fine. She'd inevitably lose her dollars and we'd find them around the house. Julie and I would return them to the allowance pile and give them back to Rose the following week. I'm pretty sure she never noticed.

Max will turn eight later this year. Until then, he gets his couple of bucks each week, sticks them in a dresser drawer, and when there are enough, heads to Target to buy Legos.

Regardless of age, we apply the same philosophy to all our kids' allowances:

Let them learn by doing.

With Rose, that means letting her treat her dollars however she wants. She won't learn that putting them under her pillow is a bad idea until she realizes she can't find them in a moment when she wants to buy something. With Max, it means letting him buy (then lose) Legos.

The same applies with our older kids. Porter (thirteen), Harrison (eleven), and Lydia (nine) each have their own YNAB budget and we let them do whatever they want with their money, under a couple of conditions. They have to:

- Set aside 10% for giving
- Put 50% of what's left after giving into savings

They can do *whatever they want* with the rest.

I have to stress how important it is to give kids this freedom, because it's the only way they'll truly learn accountability. Yes, at times your kids' entire allowance will go to Swedish Fish, but they should get the chance to make that choice. Just as we adults eventually realize limitless takeout will keep us from our goals, they'll see the same is true for candy sprees. Let them waste it. This is hard to do if you're not a wasteful person, but remember, there's just as much learning in a Swedish Fish splurge as there is in saving or giving. And isn't it better that they learn on Swedish Fish instead of something higher stakes (and more expensive)? Just try to let it go. If you're only giving them a few dollars a week, the spending will be worth the long-term learning.

Our job as parents is to guide the learning. Julie and I don't emphasize the Four Rules with the little ones but we do work on getting them to think before they spend. We keep it light-weight, with questions like "Are you sure you want that?" or "Is there anything else you might want more than that?" We don't challenge the under-eight set beyond this. When they're that little we feel it's enough to make them aware of money and start practicing.

That said, if you feel your younger kids are ready for more, go for it. It could just be an issue of numbers for Julie and me. With six kids we kind of lose steam after helping the older three with their budgets. The little ones get their cash for now and they're happy to have an allowance like their older brothers and sister. They'll get to know the Four Rules soon enough. For now it feels like enough of an accomplishment to have all six kids end the day happy and unharmed.

THE PAIN OF LETTING GO

The hardest part of teaching my kids to budget was teaching myself to let go. Once the money is theirs I fiercely believe we should not try to manage or control it for them. When Porter started budgeting after his eighth birthday,

Julie and I decided to tell him about his birthday savings. Between gifts from relatives over the years he'd accumulated about $100. We tried hard to express what a big deal it was for him to have this money. We sat on his bed and explained we'd been saving it since he was a baby, that it took years and years to accumulate this big sum. Once we thought he understood the epic proportions of this $100, we asked what he might want to do with it.

Porter immediately knew what he wanted to do: buy a LeapPad (one of the early tablets designed for kids).

I knew in my gut that this thing was not going to last. I tried telling him it didn't seem well made and that he'd probably find it boring after a while. I had such a hard time letting Porter make his own choice. My final desperate move was to give the $100 to him in singles, hoping this would make him realize just how much money it was. I thought, "Sure, once he feels it in his hands he'll want to save it."

Nope. When we got to Best Buy, Porter dropped that pile of bills in front of the cashier and skipped away with his new toy.

I wish for Porter's sake that I'd been wrong, but as suspected, he didn't end up liking the LeapPad very much. He even forgot about it after a couple of weeks.

A few months into budgeting, Porter mentioned that $100. He said that after thinking of all the things he could have done with the money, he felt he'd wasted it. He wished he'd put it toward his new-bike fund, or saved it to spend on activities with his friends. I didn't comment, because I knew he didn't need my opinion on this. It was clear the experience was going to influence his future money decisions—and that's all that mattered to me. Given that, I don't think the purchase was a waste. It was just part of Porter's (and my) growing pains.

A Word on Allowances

Before I talk about kids and the Four Rules, I want to give a bit more attention to allowances. Julie and I struggled for a while to figure out how much allowance to give to our kids. There was a period when we linked allowance to chores. The money they earned varied depending on how willing they were to do the jobs, and how well they did them.

This didn't work well. It was stressful for us because we had to quality-control every job and subjectively decide what each kid should earn for a task. The kids didn't like it, either. They never knew how much they'd earn in a given week. There was also this feeling that, gosh, if Mom is in a good mood I'll get more. If not, I'll get less. It wasn't fair to them.

Ron Lieber's advice on allowances was a breakthrough for Julie and me. When we chatted on the YNAB podcast, Ron shared his idea that allowance should not be a wage kids receive in exchange for a task accomplished. Chores are separate. They're something we do around the house because we love one another, and because we want our homes to be well functioning. We do chores as a duty and as an act of joy, love, and commitment to the people with whom we live. I completely agree with this.

Julie and I have always seen allowances as a tool for learning, but my conversation with Ron pushed our thinking on this to the next level. He pointed out that we want kids to practice with money in the same way we want them to practice their musical instruments, or practice with their art supplies. We want them to get good at money just as we want them to get good at those other things. So yanking the money if they don't do their chores doesn't make sense, in the same way it wouldn't make sense to yank their books or their violins in that situation.

I talked to Julie after interviewing Ron and we decided to announce our new allowance system that night over dinner. Chores would no longer be involved. Each kid would receive a flat amount based on his or her age. Julie and I decided on $5 for Porter and Harrison, $3 for Lydia, $2 for Max, and $1 for Rose each week. It was a big relief for us, and the kids were excited to know exactly how much they'd receive.

You have to decide what works best for your family, but I do recommend this basic approach. Treat your child's allowance as a tool for learning. Keep it consistent and keep it separate from any of their other responsibilities. With that simple system in place, you're setting the stage to teach them patience, generosity, and accountability—all qualities that will serve them well into adulthood.

Don't Worry—They'll Get It

When I tell people I start my kids on a budget at eight years old, I tend to get funny looks. I know the expressions well by now.

They're saying: *What can an eight-year-old possibly understand about expenses and priorities? Poor Mecham kids, they have to deal with their crazy YNAB drill sergeant dad.*

Crazy YNAB dad aside, we need to give all kids more credit. It's just too easy to underestimate how quickly they get it.

If we do get stuck thinking kids can't handle money or budgeting, it's often for three reasons:

We start teaching them too late.

We try teaching too much at once.

We try teaching lessons that aren't relevant to our kids' lives.

It's important to flip these roadblocks:

Start early.

Go slowly.

Stay within our kids' reality.

A middle school kid won't care about learning to prioritize bills, because she doesn't have any. But what if she's dying for an iPod Touch in February? That's way too long to wait until Christmas. Suddenly the idea of prioritizing savings will be very interesting to her.

Don't panic if you're just starting to talk to your older kids about money. The fact that you're doing this while they're still under your roof means you're doing it early! According to a U.S. Bank study, only 18% of high school seniors and undergraduate students feel their parents taught them how to manage money.[*] If you start now, whatever your kids' age, you're setting them up for success.

---

[*] U.S. Bank, "2016 U.S. Bank Student and Personal Finance Study," September 2016, https://stories.usbank.com/dam/september-2016/USBankStudentPersonal Finance.pdf.

The Four Rules Through
the Eyes of a Child

One of the first things I noticed about budgeting with kids is that they don't bring the same baggage to it that adults do. They have no concept of the (false) idea that budgeting means you're restricted or that you can't have fun. We assume our kids will share our apprehensions, but they don't. They're blank slates. All they think when looking at their budget is, "Gosh, what do I want?" They have fun thinking about it. When we adults start budgeting, we have to learn what the kids already know instinctively. Now, I get it, the stakes are much lower in a kid's budget. But realizing early that budgeting is a good thing sets kids up for a healthy relationship with money. That's a big deal.

When I start my kids on the Four Rules, each one gets a bank account and a personal budget in the YNAB software. I set up auto-transfers for their allowance so they can easily see their funds in YNAB.

If you don't use the YNAB software your kids can budget in Excel or in a notebook. You can do cash or auto-transfers. Whatever your approach, make sure they can see the money. It makes it all more real. If their allowance is in the bank, log in each week to show them their account balance. If they get cash, make sure they have it nearby when they're budgeting.

I sit down with my kids as they budget every week. Once they set aside 10% for giving and half of the rest for saving, the rest is up to them. I'm just there to encourage smart thinking. I have an effect . . . sometimes.

Deciding on priorities is the first big budgeting milestone (same for adults!). I've found that the more ideas kids have about what they want to budget for, the better the lessons once they dive into the rules. I actually spur them on if they say they want only a couple of things. "Is that *really* all you want? How about the doll you said you wanted? How about that cool watch you saw?" Their budget quickly starts looking like a letter to Santa: hoverboard, computer, watch, iPhone (Harrison nixed the iPhone when he realized he'd need to pay for the service, too). This is fine *for now.* I said earlier in the book that our budgets aren't supposed to look like holiday wish lists, but this kind of initial brainstorming is a good way to ease kids into budgeting. Remember—go slowly. If you pile on the full spectrum of possible spending, they'll get overwhelmed.

When their list is exhaustive we turn our attention to the dollars, and the Four Rules.

Not much has to change when you explain the rules to kids. But there are a few approaches you can use to help them see how each rule works in real life.

Rule One: Give Every Dollar a Job

Here's where the lengthy list comes in handy. With so many options vying for your kids' limited dollars, they immediately need to balance conflicting wants. Sound familiar? Sure, they're not balancing rent with student loans and vacation goals, but they can still see, very concretely, that money only goes so far.

That feeling of scarcity gets them focused on top priorities. They realize, "Oh gosh, I have ten things on my list but I only

really want three of them." The list of wants gets truly priori-
tized fairly quickly—they're better at it than most adults.

So with Rule One, the question for a child becomes: *What
do I want first?*

It's fascinating to watch them mull over what's important
to them. My kids inevitably decide to put all their spending
money into one category. I've never seen them spread it out
in tiny amounts over everything on the list. That's fine. The
important part is for them to look at all the options in front of
them and pick their top priorities. They're a lot better at that
than many adults I know.

You know you can't get far into Rule One without considering your true expenses. Neither can your kids. But don't
worry—they'll get this one pretty quickly, too.

Rule Two: Embrace Your True Expenses

Rules One and Two collide quickly for kids because they usually can't afford the things they want right away. If they're
budgeting with a modest allowance, they'll need to save up for
anything that's not a small fleeting purchase. Cue patience—a
lost art among many kids (and adults) today. We can all use
the practice.

Rule Two is also great for getting them to think beyond
that wish list of stuff. Remember how we define true expenses:
every expense you need to keep your life running. Kids have
these, too. They don't have the joys of car insurance or medical
deductibles, but they do have infrequent, predictable spending
goals that will sneak up on them if they don't think ahead.

Christmas and summer are perfect for explaining true expenses to kids. One is inevitably far down the road.

Our kids spend a few dollars on each other at Christmas. As they budget I remind them they may not want to have to dump all of their December allowance into gifts. So I help them calculate how much they'll need to save each month leading up to Christmas. They get excited to see their gift fund climb by summer—and they're happy to have a few extra bucks for themselves all year.

Summer is great for Rule Two because it comes with so many seasonal expenses. As parents we'll still pay for most of them (assuming allowance won't cover camp tuition or vacation costs), but kids will inevitably want to spend on things that you feel fall in their domain.

Help your kids think back to a summer experience when they wished they'd had more spending money. Do they want next summer to look different? This thinking helped Porter realize he had bigger priorities than the toys on his wish list. He goes to Scout camp in California with his cousin every year. When he came home last summer he was telling us about how lucky one kid there had been because he'd brought $20 to spend at the Scout camp store. Fast-forward to fall: Porter was set on putting all his spending money toward a hoverboard. Camp was ten months away, so I asked if he'd want to save up some spending money for the Scout store. Porter quickly figured he'd need to save $2 a month if he were to bring that coveted $20 bill to camp. He was happy to make the hoverboard wait. I've never been to that Scout camp store but it's clearly a thing of beauty.

The hoverboard did eventually make it back on Porter's list and he bought it recently with money he'd saved from working (more on that in a moment). So through a blend of budgeting and patience, he was able to have both: the spending money and the hoverboard.

As you prompt your kids to think long-term you're effectively getting them to answer the same questions you did when you started budgeting:

What do I want my money to do for me? What do I want my life to look like?

Do they want to scramble to pay for their siblings' holiday gifts, or feel excited about all the options their budget gives them for surprising their brothers and sisters? Do they want to splurge at the boardwalk arcade next summer, or relive the frustration of burning through the game money you gave them after twenty minutes of Skee-Ball?

It doesn't matter what they're spending on. The point is to build the habit of thinking long, and acting now. It will always serve them well.

Rule Two is also great for helping kids see how variable income can cover long-term expenses. Todd and Jessica budget with their kids Sadie (fourteen), Wyeth (eleven), and Oliver (nine). Sadie earns a wildly variable income—some months it's just allowance, other months she makes a killing taking care of their neighbors' ducks and flowers while they're away. When Todd and Jessica got Sadie her first phone, it came with a big lesson on managing income. The device was a gift and Todd and Jessica also paid for 100% of the first few months of service. After that, Sadie was responsible for 25% and then eventually 50% of her monthly bill. Sadie's immediate reaction to paying 50% was that it was more money than she "made" each month. But what about the duck windfalls? When Todd pointed out that she could spread those earnings over multiple months, it clicked. Rule Two went into full effect in Sadie's budget.

Rule Three: Roll with the Punches

You know how I said kids don't bring the same baggage to budgeting that adults do? This is especially true for Rule Three. As adults, we often have to remind ourselves that changing our budget isn't failure. It's just life. Kids are way more resilient. Once they understand that their dollars can go only so far, they are fairly open to working within those parameters.

If my kids want to buy something outside their budget I try to remind them they'll need to shift their dollars to fit in the purchase. They're usually quick to decide: nix the new thing or shift their priorities. They never see it as failure—they're just changing their minds about their priorities. Awhile back, Todd's son Oliver was saving up for a few different toys (Legos, Minion figures, Pokémon cards, and a couple of other top priorities—hey, he's nine). During a visit to the aquarium Oliver zeroed in on an $11 stuffed penguin at the gift shop. He had no stuffed-penguin budget so he asked Todd if he'd buy it for him. Todd said no, but he pulled out Oliver's budget on his phone so Oliver could see what he might want to move into a new-penguin category. It was Rule Three *in advance*, which is the best kind. Oliver adjusted his budget because his priorities changed, and he didn't have to wait for the overspending to happen. The penguin was his—and he still sleeps with it every night.

Again, I know the stakes are wildly different for kids. There's just no comparing the choice between a penguin and Pokémon to shifting your dollars to cover groceries. But they're working the same skills. All that practice will prepare them for the day when rolling with the punches means so much more than playing with their allowance.

I mentioned back in Chapter 4 that the analogy for Roll with the Punches comes from boxing. When your opponent throws a punch, it will hurt a lot less if you move with the blow. You're also less likely to get hit (as hard). Well, imagine entering the boxing ring for the first time as an adult. You know the rules, but wow, it's not easy. Now imagine entering that ring after practicing the bob-and-weave since childhood. It will still be challenging, but you'd be so agile you'd barely break a sweat. That will be your kid in a few years. A budgeting prodigy.

For now, all that your kids need to know is that it's okay to change their budget. But they'll already know this. We're the ones who need the constant reminding.

Rule Four: Age Your Money

Okay, fine: your kids probably don't worry about breaking the paycheck-to-paycheck cycle. (They're wise beyond their years if they do. Now tell them to go outside and play.) It's still worth getting Rule Four on their radar, though. Like the other rules, it's good practice for later years. And for now, it's simply a fun measure to see how well they're doing.

Awhile back, Harrison asked what "Age of Money" meant in the top corner of the YNAB software. He's our big saver, so it showed that his money was 250 days old (this kid basically never spends his allowance). I explained that, on average, the dollar he spends today was earned 250 days ago. He thought this was pretty cool, so he went to Lydia and Porter to ask what their age of money was (way lower). It became a bragging thing for him, which I don't totally support, but I secretly enjoyed seeing how proud he was of his progress. Don't tell his siblings.

If you're budgeting offline, you can calculate age of money by dividing the total money on hand by the amount your kids typically spend in a month. This can get tricky if their spending is variable, but it still gives you a general idea. So, if they spend $20 a month and have $100 on hand, their age of money is about five months.

At this point Rule Four is mostly a fun exercise. But it won't hurt for our kids to get excited about seeing their money age. If they get in that mindset now, it may keep them from getting pulled into a paycheck-to-paycheck life when the stakes are real. Or at worst, they'll have the tools to kill the stress if expenses do get overwhelming. What a gift that would be.

WHEN OUR KIDS KEEP US IN CHECK

Recently my friend Maria and her husband, Joe, decided they'd start saving for a dog. They don't budget with their five-year-old son, Luca, but they did share the plan with him. He was thrilled, although he didn't want to wait. "We know we want a dog. Why can't we get it today?" he asked.

Maria and Joe explained that dogs come with big expenses: food, vet care, boarding if they ever wanted to take a trip. They wanted to save at least $1,000 before getting the dog so they'd be prepared to take care of it. "But on the bright side," Joe said, "we can save that money quickly if we don't buy little things we don't need."

Luca completely got this—so much so that he started policing his parents' spending. Their next grocery run was a full-on interrogation: "Mama, do you really need that hummus? Don't we already have peanut butter at home? You said last time that avocados are so expensive. You can save that money for our dog!"

To be fair, Luca was willing to make his own sacrifices. He offered to give up the $0.88 Hot Wheels car he'd sometimes get as a reward for being good at the grocery store. He also volunteered to skip Pizza Friday, the one day he bought lunch at school. Even without his own budget this kid was rocking priorities like a boss.

The family's "Brutus Fund" (Luca already named the dog) is due to fill up by summer, just in time for Luca to learn how to scoop poop from the lawn. Meanwhile, he's eased up on his parents a bit—Maria gets to indulge in avocados *sometimes*. Luca's eagerness also motivated his parents to cut spending more than they'd planned. Skipping three date nights saved a couple hundred dollars and they've put a ban on takeout until Brutus can be there to nag for scraps. With Luca on the case, they may even hit their goal by spring.

Who Pays for What?

When you start your older kids on a budget, it's good to be clear up front about what they're expected to pay for. This can get tricky if they've gotten used to you paying for things. You don't want them to feel they're being punished if their cash supply is suddenly being cut off. This is meant to be fun. Plus, you're still giving them money—only now, they can do *whatever they want* with it. They don't even need to ask you.

I suggest having a budget meeting with your kids, just like you would a spouse or partner, to decide what things are their responsibility and what you will continue to provide. You can also decide to share expenses. The parameters are totally up to you and they can evolve as your kids grow.

Todd and Jessica talk with their kids about how much they need to budget for savings, gifts, and for giving. Other than that, just like our kids, the category choices are theirs.

Todd and Jessica are willing to help the kids pay for experiences, like rock climbing with friends, but not stuff. The kids are free to budget for whatever they want with their own money, which empowers them to buy things that their parents otherwise wouldn't (Pokémon cards, beloved stuffed penguin, whatever).

They also decide together what expenses they'll share. Todd and Jessica agreed to pay for 50% of Sadie's phone bill because they feel it's truly a shared expense. They want to be able to reach Sadie when she's out just as much as—maybe more than—Sadie wants the phone for herself (she is the rare teenager who is not phone obsessed).

Wyeth saves up for cycling gear, but most of it is so expensive that Todd and Jessica help him cover the costs. Different families will have different choices about what parents will fund, what kids will fund, and what is in between. But like Todd's kids, they can all develop the habit of budgeting and gain the experience they need to prioritize.

Once your kids have part-time jobs, they can gradually take on more expenses that you feel fall in their domain. Porter, Harrison, and Lydia did this when they started working at YNAB.

Yes, the thirteen-, eleven-, and nine-year-old work at YNAB. They share the glamorous job of cleaning the office.

After the kids were budgeting with more than a few dollars, Julie and I decided they should take more ownership over gifting. We got the idea at a time when they'd attended about six birthday parties in a month between the three of them. We were getting gift fatigue, so we floated the idea of having them use their money for their friends' gifts. They were totally up for it.

Now they have total control over their friends' and siblings' birthday gifts. They get excited thinking about what to buy, and even spy for clues on what a friend might like when they're hanging out. They'd barely thought about it before. Julie or I would just pick up a gift while running errands. Paying for it themselves has made them more thoughtful gifters. It's fun to watch as a parent.

Remember that the overarching goal is to teach our kids how to handle money well. Don't get too hung up on drawing a line between who pays for what. It's good to have a clear system in place, but the bigger picture is way more important.

This Is What Happens When You Let a Teenager Do Whatever She Wants with Her Money

Our oldest kid is thirteen years old at the time of this writing. That means our grand experiment to raise financially responsible young adults is still in beta. But if Jon Dale's family is any indication, I think the kids will be all right.

Jon's daughter Anna is seventeen years old. She loves Korean pop music and has pink hair. She's a talented visual artist. She works in a movie theater and has been using YNAB since she was hired at fifteen. Anna needed no convincing when it came to budgeting, despite the fact that her parents paid for all of her spending before she got a job.

"I started using YNAB because my parents use it," she explains. "I was also concerned about entering life without having any way to manage my money. When I started working, I wanted to pay for my own things. I buy a lot of my own clothes now and when I'm buying superfluous things I like to use my own money."

Jon helped Anna set up her budget when she got her first paycheck. Since then she calls him only when she needs backup. Recently her account balance was off by $100 (she had more in the bank than her budget balance showed) and Jon helped her figure it out. Aside from encouraging Anna to put some money toward giving, Jon and his wife, Amy, give her free rein over her budget.

Jon recalls a night a few months ago when Anna came home from the mall with her friends. When he asked what she'd bought, she said she didn't get anything. Her specific words were, "I don't have money available right now." *Interesting.*

Jon can see Anna's bank account, since it's linked to his. He knew she had a few thousand dollars in there at the time. How can a teenager be set free in a mall with thousands to her name and not spend a thing?

Priorities. Anna has lots, and it happens that she can't fulfill any of them by buying stuff at the mall. These are her budget categories right now:

Giving
  Giving
Everyday Expenses
  Spending money
  Restaurants
  Clothing
  Makeup

Rainy Day Funds
  Emergency fund
  Birthdays
  Christmas
  Cosplay
  RAOK (random acts of kindness)
Long-Term Spending
  Korean lessons
  Savings goals
  Car
  Concert savings
  Crazy hair
  Travel

One of Anna's biggest—and most expensive—priorities is her love for K-pop music. And by that I don't mean she likes watching K-pop videos on YouTube. She funds her own concert tickets and travel to see K-pop shows. She recently went to Dallas for a concert. Anna wants to go to art school in Korea, so she also funds her own Korean language lessons throughout the year.

After seeing Anna's budget, it's clear why she doesn't turn a trip to the mall into a spending blitz. Nothing in those shop windows can compare to the exciting priorities that are waiting for her dollars. As Anna puts it, "I'd rather have amazing experiences than own a bunch of crap." Can't argue with that.

TEACHING YOUR KIDS TO BUDGET

Don't listen to the naysayers—kids can budget! Teaching your kids to be smart with money is one of the greatest gifts you can give them. As you get them started, remember:

- **Use allowances as tools for learning.** We want kids to practice getting good at money, just as we'd want them to work at building any other life skill. Taking away their allowance (for whatever reason) is just as bad as taking away their books or their musical instruments. Keep the learning going no matter what.
- Don't underestimate how quickly kids get it. They *will* keep up with budgeting as long as you **start early**, **go slowly**, and **stay within their reality**.
- The Four Rules are just as relevant to kids as they are to adults. Just keep the conversation at their level and give them the freedom to **learn by doing**.
- Sit down with your kids and **set a clear framework for who pays for what expenses in your life**. There are no set rules, of course, as long as your plan works for you.

CHAPTER 9:

When You Feel Like Quitting

There's something important you need to know about me: I love doughnuts.

I love them so much, I almost quit budgeting over them.

What? It was a moment of weakness.

I'd mentioned earlier that when Julie and I started budgeting, things were super-tight. Full-time student. Hourly social worker. Bus pass. Basement apartment. Coupon maven. It was challenging, but we were so dead set on staying out of debt and saving for future kids, we gave ourselves no choice but to make it work. Every spending decision was obsessively planned. There was no room for anything beyond our basic needs and obligations.

It worked well enough for a few months. Then one day during my walk to class I passed a bakery that makes amazing doughnuts. I remember staring at this one chocolate glazed beauty in the display case and wanting it so badly. But I couldn't buy it. We had zero budget for any kind of eating out. This doughnut was $0.50 and I didn't have the money. It was so depressing.

I'd felt the same way a couple of weeks earlier when I missed dinner while studying late at the library. I remember walking by the vending machines where they sold $1 cookies. I didn't have the money and I recall thinking, "Well, I just won't eat anything tonight." I knew this was ridiculous even then. A budget should never make you feel that eating is not an option.

I pushed past the dinner incident, but the doughnut just broke me.

I tried hard not to say anything to Julie for a while. Budgeting had been my idea, and yet she was so much better at being frugal than I was. But I knew I couldn't keep going. We had no breathing room. It felt like any unplanned purchase would make the whole budget implode.

I eventually did tell Julie and she was right there with me. Turns out she'd nearly broken down over a missed connection with a croissant the week before. (Our love for baked goods unites us.) That's when we decided to budget that $5 fun money I talked about earlier. It was so tiny, but it was all we needed to lose the feeling that our budget might collapse with a single move. Plus, looking at it another way, $5 was ten doughnuts a month. I never took it that far, but just knowing that I could . . . oh, the freedom.

You're going to want to quit budgeting. Whether you crack over something as small as a doughnut or as epic as a major unexpected expense, it will happen at some point. Money will feel impossibly tight. Expenses will seem beyond your control. Tracking every transaction will feel like an exercise in futility.

I'm ending this book with a chapter on quitting because it's such a normal part of budgeting. The temptation to quit will come up, but if you've read this far and you're even settling in to read this chapter, I'm betting you don't actually want to stop budgeting. Perhaps it's just feeling too difficult. The chocolate doughnut is staring back at you and you're dying for a way to buy it. (Sorry, was that just me?)

I've found that when most of us want to quit, it's because we're caught up in self-sabotaging behaviors that are actually pretty simple to fix. All it takes is a little investigating to figure out why your budget isn't working for you.

The Perfect Budget Fail

Most of our reasons for wanting to quit budgeting stem from one core problem: perfection. When we feel we're failing, it's often because we're pushing too hard for a perfect budget.

Perfection likes to wear disguises, but it's at the root of nearly every budgeting pitfall. It's self-inflicted to boot, which is actually a good thing (although it doesn't sound like it). Once you're aware of the behaviors that kill your chances of success, you can do something to counter them.

To start, beware of the common notion that a budget is binary. We tend to fall into the trap of seeing our budget as black or white: failure or success. That's simply not true. As long as you're budgeting, you're succeeding. Do whatever you need to do to remember this (you can also add it to your other mantra, "debt is not an option"). I promise it will set you free.

Then keep an eye out for these lurking budget behaviors. They're all ways in which we push for that elusive perfection, usually without realizing it. If you see yourself in any of these, know that you *can* easily get yourself unstuck. The solution is actually the same for every one of these: step back and think of what you can do to make things easier on yourself. Really.

Not leaving yourself breathing room. Also known as the doughnut incident. This is one of the most common behaviors that make people want to quit. It makes sense to limit spending when money is tight, but you can do this only to a point. If you don't have at least a little bit of give, everything will eventually break (your sanity, your budget, your resolve . . .).

I'm big into weight lifting and this idea of extra give reminds me of having a spotter when bench pressing. You could be buried under a barbell, sure the thing is about to crush your chest, when your spotter uses two index fingers to barely pull up on the bar and help you complete the lift. That bit of help means the difference between failure and success.

No matter how tight things feel, leave room for your proverbial doughnut. Have a spotter standing by in case you need that tiny lift. Just a few dollars a month can save you from feeling that everything is going to come crashing down.

Setting unrealistic spending targets. This is very common when you start budgeting, especially because you lack the data you need to set realistic spending goals. If you've never tracked your grocery spending, how can you know whether that $300 target is anywhere near your reality? It may sound reasonable, but if you typically spend $800 a month it will take time and discipline to get there. And maybe your realistic target isn't actually $300, and you get frustrated trying to reach it every month, when instead $450 might be reasonable for your family.

Assuming rapid change. Perhaps you've realized you spend $800 a month on groceries. Good! You're now working with real numbers. But trouble brews if you swear you'll only spend $300 starting *today*. It's a great goal but you can't expect to change your behavior overnight—especially by such a huge degree. The same goes for your partner if you're not budgeting solo. We often expect the other person to change rapidly, but they won't. Even if you do hit your new goal once or twice, meaningful change takes time. Be kind to yourself (and to your partner). Set realistic goals and work your way toward them slowly.

This advice stands even if you don't have all the cash you need to cover your expenses. If that's the case, yes, tighten spending however you reasonably can, but also realize that changing your spending behavior alone—however quickly—won't solve your problem. If there's a gap between your income and expenses, you need to find ways to bring in more money. There are stories throughout the book of how others have done this. You're sure to be overwhelmed if you put all your focus on hitting unrealistic spending targets overnight. It's best to use a combination of smarter spending *and* earning.

Demanding too much of yourself. I've made the comparison between budgeting and diet/exercise before. There's a way in which the similarities can't be ignored. In both scenarios, you will burn out if you demand too much of yourself (this is really true in all areas of life). You're overdoing it when you obsess over your budget, check it several times a day, and talk about it to anyone who will give you an ear. You'll fizzle out, just as you would after an intense period of calorie counting and daily gym visits. Treat your budget or your healthy habits like a fad and they'll disappear like one. Work on integrating them into your real life and they will become your actual lifestyle.

It's great if you're *really* into your budget (it is a thing of beauty, I know!), but try to keep it from consuming you. Check in every few days. Make sure you're staying on track. Then go on living your life.

The OCD factor. Bet you didn't think there were so many ways to go crazy over your budget. . . . When the budgeting OCD kicks in, you just can't let the penny go. And you *will* need to let the penny go at some point. A (hopefully) small transaction will hit your account that you can't, for the life of you, remember. You can drive yourself nuts trying to figure it out, or assign it to a spending area that has available funds and move on.

A subset of budgeting OCD is trying to be too granular. If you've never in your life tracked your spending and suddenly want to track each tube of toothpaste, your budget won't be sustainable. Sure, break your spending into categories like groceries, utilities, etc., but don't get lost in the weeds with every little item. Unless one transaction very clearly straddles two spending targets (like when one Costco receipt covers food *and* skis *and* pajama pants), send it to one category and be at peace.

Complexity. A person with one credit card and one bank account will undoubtedly have an easier time budgeting than someone with several of each. Nix unnecessary complexity by closing extra bank accounts or routing your money to just one or two accounts. If you're juggling multiple credit cards, use the one with the lowest fees and/or best perks (ahem, when you have the cash on hand to spend!). Pay off balances if you have them and use only that one card moving forward.

I know sticking with budgeting won't always be as simple as assigning $5 for doughnut money. Some setbacks will feel so insurmountable, so out of your control, that quitting will seem like the only option. But nothing is insurmountable. Even if you're overwhelmed by a sudden expense or income cut, your budget will work as long as you let it flex with you. Who cares if it looks nothing like you'd hoped when you started budgeting? Progress will happen as long as you keep being intentional with your dollars. Maybe it means you're not as close to your goals as you'd hoped, but quitting will guarantee that they'll stay out of reach. Remember: When things feel too difficult, think of what you can do to make your life easier. Then focus on *that*.

Don't Forget That Little Thing Called Happiness

We can blame perfection for most budget pitfalls. Keyword: **most**. Sometimes, though, we're tempted to quit because we've lost sight of the point. We get so entrenched in paying bills and hitting spending targets that we forget why we're budgeting in the first place.

Remember, your budget is there to help you create the life you want, now and in the future. Budgeting isn't about delaying your happiness. If it were, nobody would stick to it for long. When you're happy, you're motivated. You feel you're moving toward your goals, and that momentum makes you want to work harder. That's when the magic happens—but it's not really magic; it's just you, operating at your fullest potential.

If you're not happy with your budget, go back to the question you asked yourself on page 3:

What do I want my money to do for me?

This will bring you perspective. You may find that your budget *is* still moving you toward the life you want. Perhaps slower than you'd hoped, but you're still going in the right direction. That refresher may be enough to restore your mindset.

If you realize your money is *not* doing what you want, go back to Rule One. Or even better, wipe out your whole budget and start over. Forget every obligation and goal, so it's just you and your checking account balance again. With that blank slate, go back again to the big question: *What do I want my money to do for me?*

All Hail the Fresh Start

I'm a big advocate of the budget do-over. It's so important to take a step back at times to make sure your money is doing what you want it to do. This is the furthest thing from quitting. Restarting is victory. You're killing it if you restart. I believe this so strongly, I've worked a Fresh Start feature into the YNAB software. When things get stale, or you feel your budget just isn't working for you anymore, I hope you'll wipe it out and start over—whether that means clicking the Fresh Start link or opening a new notebook or spreadsheet.

Restarting your budget is not very different from the kind of introspective thinking we often do around New Year's. It's a time to reflect on your purpose and see how your actions align with it, then make adjustments as needed. When you restart your budget, you're also thinking deeply about your life—only now you're considering how your money can help you get to where you want to go.

Remember Phil and Alexis from Chapter 1? When you first met them Alexis was about to jump the corporate ship to launch her career as a freelance Web designer. I caught up with them a year later to find out how their new adventure was going.

Turns out it's been going exactly, and not at all, as planned.

The good: Six months after quitting her job, Alexis had more work opportunities than she could ever accept. This was, of course, a big relief. Before quitting she had worried about how she'd keep her pipeline full. She didn't expect that so many of her former colleagues and clients would refer her for projects. It was a pleasant by-product of having built solid relationships at her last job, and being great at what she does.

The tricky: Alexis could have easily doubled her old salary by taking every project. But a bigger workload would have meant round-the-clock hours. The point of going freelance was for Alexis to spend more time with their son, Jack. The lure of more money did not override her top priority: family. It felt strange turning down lucrative job opportunities, but she and

Phil agreed that family balance was more important than extra cash. . . .

The bad: But they could have really used that extra cash. They weren't in dire straits but their income was not keeping up with their spending. With Alexis's variable income, she'd jump from bringing in nothing one month to depositing a $10,000 check the next. They tried spreading the big payments over several months but they *always* went over budget. A check that they'd intended to last them four months barely made it to three.

Budgeting helped, but it was also a rude awakening every time they opened that spreadsheet. They both hated seeing how quickly the dollars got swallowed. It became so overwhelming, they started to believe they'd be happier without a budget. They thought that maybe if they just took a breath and stopped thinking about money so much, things would work themselves out.

The First Solution: Budget Detox

As much as Phil and Alexis wanted to kill the budget and bask in ignorance, they knew that wouldn't be smart. They also knew they had to change *something* about their current setup. So if dropping the budget wasn't the answer, they'd do the opposite: start over.

Usually a restart just involves putting away your old budget and starting a new one. Simply looking at all of your money as a clean slate, nothing attached to any jobs, is a powerful exercise. That's what Phil and Alexis eventually did, but first Alexis wanted to get ruthless on their old budget. They'd already done a version of this last year when trying to stretch their freelance fund, but it was time for another checkup. Alexis felt their new budget would be stronger if she could identify the weaknesses in the old one—and get rid of them. She wanted to look under the hood on every single expense. Here's what she found:

Natural gas: Their last two gas bills were over $150. A quick look back showed that the same bills were less than $100 during the same time last year. What the? They were even running on a brand-new furnace. Perhaps this year was colder, or maybe they overestimated the new furnace's fuel efficiency. Whatever the reason, Alexis wanted to kill that extra $50. The plan: lower the thermostat a few degrees at night and snuggle up in flannel everything. They also started using their thermostat's timer so they wouldn't forget to adjust the temperature. It worked. The next month their bill was $53 lower.

Cell phones: This category stung. They were paying $145 a month for their two smartphones. They had to do better, but downgrading to the cheapest data plan only saved them $20 a month. Switching meant ponying up hundreds on new phones. The math didn't make sense. They felt stuck and duped by their modern lives. So, more sleuthing. Alexis discovered a far less expensive cell phone provider through one of her favorite money bloggers, Mr. Money Mustache. While they each did need to spend $250 on new phones, their new $46 bill (*total for two phones*) made it worth it. With $99 in monthly savings, they'd cover the cost of their new phones after five months.

Karate: They'd signed up Jack for karate last year using a Groupon. Twenty dollars for eight classes and a free uniform.

Score! Jack loves all things ninja, so he was in heaven. When the Groupon expired, Alexis went to lock in regular enrollment. She's still not sure how she didn't fall over when she saw the price: $150 a month. For a four-year-old to do karate?! Oh, but Jack was so happy on the mat. She quickly started justifying the price. *We'll skip two dinners out each month. I'll cancel the gym membership I never use.* Fast-forward one year: Jack was on his way to a junior brown belt, but he'd spent the last month finding excuses for skipping class. He just never wanted to go anymore. The dojo requires autopay, so they paid that $150 whether or not Jack went to class. Easy decision: cancel for now. They could always go back if Jack wanted to. But in the two months since canceling, Jack never asked once to go to karate.

Cable: Phil was ready to go cold turkey on the TV. They could save $80 a month by canceling cable. Netflix plus Hulu were enough to keep them entertained. When Phil called to cancel, he was promptly offered a $30 discount on their bill *and* a few premium channels for free—way better than the expensive package they'd downgraded from last year. He put them on hold for a quick powwow with Alexis, and then took the deal. Sure, they'd only be saving $30 instead of $80, but they figured the extra movie channels were good for date nights in. They could still cancel later if they wanted to save more. Meanwhile, they're opting out of Netflix ($10) and Hulu ($12), so the total savings are $52.

Groceries: This was a huge point of stress for Alexis. She didn't get it: How could three people (really, two and a half) eat through $500 in groceries each month? They'd never tracked their grocery spending before they started budgeting, but they thought $300 a month would be more than enough. Alexis did the grocery shopping and she felt like a failure every month.

The challenge was that their grocery game was already supertight. Healthy eating was a huge priority for them both, which translated to hardly any junk in their grocery cart. They mostly bought fresh produce and high-quality protein, plus Jack's other staples: milk, pasta, bread, Cheerios. Coupons didn't help much since they're mostly for processed foods, which rarely hit their cart.

Alexis's solution was similar to what Julie and I did in this scenario. She decided to add more to their grocery spending in the new budget and stop stressing. A year's worth of budget data proved that eating well simply cost more than she'd thought. She still planned to eye the sales and avoid unnecessary spending, but she was going to stop treating their grocery spending like a big mystery.

Disney: They'd saved $4,000 over the last ten months so they could surprise Jack with a trip to Disney World for his fifth birthday. Phil and Alexis both looked at this lump of money now and had to ask themselves: *Who the heck cares about Disney?* Jack certainly didn't. He liked Mickey well enough, but he was still at the age where a bucket of Hot Wheels and a trip to the beach made him plenty happy. He was by no means asking for a fancy vacation. The more they thought about it, the trip was a parenting bucket list item for them more than a request from Jack. They'd be much happier using that money to relieve cash-flow stress right now. Plus, if they waited a couple of years Jack would be tall enough to actually ride Splash Mountain. It was a no-brainer: no Disney for now.

Bottom line: Alexis's sleuthing saved them about $251 a month ($351 at first, then she added $100 to groceries), plus the $4,000 that was tied up in the Disney trip. Not a life-changing solution, but knowing that they'd freed up some cash helped with morale. They were moving in the right direction and were motivated to keep going.

The Second Solution:
Earn More Money

Something nagged Alexis every time she turned down a project inquiry. She knew she didn't have time to take on the work herself, but maybe she didn't have to. She'd always dreamed of expanding her one-woman operation into a mini design studio. She could partner with up-and-coming designers by subcontracting projects to them and overseeing their work. They'd all win: Alexis could earn extra income as art director while her junior colleagues built their portfolios.

She'd always thought this dream would be years away. But why did it have to be? She had three unanswered job inquiries in her in-box right now. Just the week before, she'd had coffee with her former assistant, Elena, who'd said she was drowning in administrative tasks at work. She wished she had more opportunities to flex her design muscles.

Alexis had mentored Elena for three years. She knew Elena had talent, and that she was totally reliable. After a quick text exchange, it was on: Elena was excited to be considered for any upcoming projects. Alexis replied to the three pending inquiries in her in-box. She would start her new role as art director—and ignite a new income stream—as soon as she lined up her next project.

The Restart

With expenses down and a new income stream coming soon, Phil and Alexis felt reenergized. Staying within their budget would still require daily effort, but they were motivated just knowing that their bills and cash flow were optimized. Every dollar was going exactly where they wanted, or needed, it to go—and nowhere else. Here's a look at their before-and-after budget.

Phil and Alexis's Post-Detox Budget
BILLS Mortgage: $2,500 **Natural gas: $100** Electricity: $70 Car payment: $275 Preschool: $800 Internet: $40 **Cable: $50** ~~Netflix/Hulu: $0~~ A's life insurance: $55 **Cell phones $46** ~~Karate $0~~ BILLS TOTAL: $3,936

EVERYDAY SPENDING
Groceries: $600
Household supplies: $50
Fuel: $120
Work expenses: $100
Restaurants/fun: $75
Babysitter: $100
ED SPENDING TOTAL: $1,045

GOALS
~~Disney: $0~~

TRUE EXPENSES
Car insurance: $120
Car repairs: $50
Health/medical: $50
Water: $60
Birthdays/holidays: $40
Basement repairs: $150
TRUE EXPENSES TOTAL: $470

The Bonus

Alexis loves geeking out on money. Reading the *Wall Street Journal* brings her joy. Warren Buffett is a personal hero. She and Phil save for retirement but she has always wished she could open a general investment account and try her hand at some exchange-traded funds, or ETFs. She's just never felt they had the extra money to justify it.

Now that she and Phil were more in control of their budget, she was motivated to launch her little investing dream—and she wouldn't even dip into the budget. Her plan was to sell the stuff they didn't use. Every dollar earned went straight into their investment account. She started with $15 after consigning her copy of *Alexander Hamilton* at the local used bookstore. Small balance aside, she was officially in the market! It gave her such a thrill.

She had no extra time to put into selling (work! Jack! Phil!), so she stuck to two easy outlets: consigning books at her neighborhood store and selling on Facebook "online yard sales." With a photo and quick description, she made $350 on Facebook selling a gently used stove that the previous homeowners had left in their basement. She made another $40 selling a wagon that Jack never used. Another $390 into the investment account!

WHEN YOU FEEL LIKE QUITTING

Y ou *will* want to quit budgeting at some point—and that's okay. When it happens, just think of ways you can make things easier on yourself. Also be aware of the most common budgeting pitfalls (they happen to the best of us):

- Not leaving yourself breathing room. Must buy doughnuts.
- Setting unrealistic spending targets. Your efforts may be noble, but they won't work if they don't fit your real life.
- Assuming rapid change. Take it slow.
- Demanding too much of yourself. Be kind.
- Getting OCD on your budget. Let the little things go.
- Complexity. Keep it simple.

When all else fails, you may need a budget reset. Erase the whole thing and start fresh: Write new goals and spending targets, and then assign your dollars. Bring it all back to that life-changing question: *What do I want my money to do for me?*

You've Got This

If you walk away with nothing else from this book, I hope you'll realize that budgeting is not restrictive. It's quite the opposite. When you budget with YNAB's Four Rules, you're in total control of your financial circumstances. You're designing your life around your priorities, and nothing feels better than hitting your goals, no matter how long it may take.

If you don't have a budget already, I hope you'll try it. Be patient and remember that most important goals can't be achieved overnight. But small changes make a big difference.

When you're feeling discouraged, just think of where you'd like to be three months, six months, or a year from now. Keep budgeting, even if it's not perfect (it never will be!), and don't look back. You'll be amazed at what you can accomplish.

You can do this. Today. Right now.

What do you have to lose? Except all that debt and stress. (Okay, so kind of a lot.)

You've got this.

Acknowledgments

This book was a group effort, and would not have been possible without the work of so many people along the way:

Julie, my wife, for supporting me ever since I first uttered the phrase, "I think we need a budget."

Taylor Brown, my business partner and YNAB CTO, for his careful consideration coupled with unflinching confidence.

Todd Curtis, YNAB CCO, for his ability to get from vague idea to crystal clear concept.

Lindsey Burgess, YNAB CMO, for her enthusiasm for this project from day one.

Lauren Coulsen, YNAB designer, for her fantastic cover design and illustration work.

Maria Gagliano, writer, for her determination to get everything I've ever written or recorded synthesized into an actual book.

Lisa DiMona, book agent extraordinaire, for taking a chance on me and teaching me all along the way.

Stephanie Hitchcock and the HarperCollins team, for all of their work in bringing YNAB to the world.

The entire YNAB team, for their dogged persistence in helping people align their money with their priorities.

YNABers everywhere, for their continued enthusiasm in sharing YNAB with their friends and family.

Where to Read, Watch, and Listen to All Things YNAB

If you're rolling on the budget love and want to keep going, our friend the Internet won't let you down. New resources and communities crop up all the time, so this is just a sample of the many great things out there.

Learning Tools at YNAB.com

Free Classes: We post new classes regularly, all free, and you don't need to subscribe to the YNAB software to access them. We keep them small so you can get your questions answered, and each one is run by a YNAB budgeting expert. Here's a snapshot of the classes offered at the time of this writing:

- Master Credit Cards with Your Budget
- Aggressive Debt Paydown
- Reach Your Savings Goals
- Break the Paycheck-to-Paycheck Cycle
- Pay for Big Expenses Without Borrowing
- Budgeting When Broke
- Take Control of Your Food Budget

Visit https://www.youneedabudget.com/classes/ for the latest schedule.

Weekly videos: I riff on new budget topics every week in my White-board Wednesday videos. You can subscribe at https://www.youtube .com/YouNeedABudget.

The YNAB podcast: If you prefer to just *hear* me and not *see* me, the YNAB podcast has you covered. Find it by searching for YNAB on iTunes or visit https://soundcloud.com/iynab.

Blog: We talk budgeting on the blog nearly every day. Get your reading on at https://www.youneedabudget.com/blog/.

Weekly newsletter: The *YNAB Weekly Roundup* is always short, informative, and inspirational. Because who wants emails that are anything but that? You can sign up at https://www.youneedabudget .com/weekly-roundup/.

Guides: Browse through our guides for a jolt of inspiration—and useful how-tos—on the Four Rules and other big budgeting topics at https://www.youneedabudget.com/guides/.

Around the Web

We're humbled by the amazing YNAB communities that our fans have created. I'm sure I'm missing some, because the Internet is in-finite, but at the time of this writing some of the busiest YNAB fan communities are here:

Facebook Groups
YNAB Fans: https://www.facebook.com/groups/YNABFans/

Friendly YNAB Support: https://www.facebook.com/groups /1401727190120850/

YNAB Subreddit
https://www.reddit.com/r/ynab/

You can also find us on Facebook (facebook.com/iYNAB/), Insta-gram (@youneedabudget), and Twitter (@YNAB).

Index

About the Author

JESSE MECHAM is the founder and CEO of You Need a Budget (YNAB), a software and education company that helps people align their money with their priorities. While still a college student, very broke and newly married, Jesse developed a system for budgeting that worked. He thought maybe he could sell his system on the Internet to help cover his $400-a-month rent. It turns out he wasn't the only one who needed a budget. Over a decade later, YNAB has helped hundreds of thousands of people break the paycheck-to-paycheck cycle, get out of debt, and save more money. When he's not teaching people how to budget, Jesse loves gardening, CrossFit, and travel. He also spends a good bit of time with his wife, Julie, and the six small people who live in their home.